OPTIMAL INVESTING

OPTIMAL INVESTING

How To *Protect* and *Grow* Your Wealth With Asset Allocation

SCOTT P. FRUSH, CFA, CFP

MRP

Marshall Rand Publishing
Royal Oak, Michigan

 For information, address Marshall Rand Publishing, P.O. Box 1849, Royal Oak, MI 48068-1849.
Email: Contact@MarshallRand.com.

Printed in the United States of America.

Frush, Scott P.
Optimal investing: how to protect and grow your wealth with asset allocation/Scott Frush

ISBN 0-9744374-3-3

Library of Congress Control Number 2003111333

Books from Marshall Rand Publishing may be purchased at special quantity discounts. For more information please write: Marshall Rand Publishing, Special Promotions, P.O. Box 1849, Royal Oak, MI 48068-1849.

This book is dedicated to

Michael, Todd and Jason

CONTENTS

Acknowledgements

There are a number of people I would like to thank who helped make this book possible. Special thanks goes to Howard Katz, Jennifer Maxwell, John Northcott, Christina Fallone, Michael Dudkowski, Mark Waugh, Timothy Hutton and Jason Frush for their valuable insights and helpful recommendations.

Many sincere thanks to Scott Theiring for his tireless assistance and critical review. Also, a word of gratitude goes to Richard Mazel of 41 North Partners for his insights and counsel.

For such an exceptional cover design I'd like to thank Cathi Stevenson of Book Cover Express. For their outstanding mentoring and guidance early in my career I'd like to thank John Nixon, Ronald Miller and Jay Fishman. Lastly, I'd like to express my sincere thanks to Dan Poynter and Jerrold Jenkins for their expert advice on how to turn my vision into this book.

Scott Frush

Introduction

"A successful investor was a novice investor who followed the right approach."

– Scott Frush

◆ ◆ ◆

What is Optimal Investing? In many ways, Optimal Investing *is* the right approach. With the right approach, the novice investor becomes the successful investor.

Not all approaches to wealth building and wealth preservation produce the same results, or worse yet even work. Some are clearly better than the rest. This is the heart of Optimal Investing. In practice, I define Optimal Investing as the strategy of employing time-honored and research backed principles and practices to protect and grow an investor's wealth within the context of his or her objectives and constraints. One of the principal ways Optimal Investing accomplishes this objective is to build an investor's optimal portfolio. An optimal portfolio is a portfolio that provides the highest expected total rate of return given the level of risk an investor is willing and able to assume in order to achieve his or her specific financial goals.

What Optimal Investing Does Emphasize	What Optimal Investing Does NOT Emphasize
Asset allocation over security selection and market timing	Security selection and market timing over asset allocation
Protecting and growing wealth	Only growing wealth
Long-term investing	Playing the market
Maximizing expected total return for a given level of risk	Maximizing expected total return without regard to risk
Incorporating the majority of asset classes and asset subclasses	Incorporating only those asset classes and asset subclasses with strong recent returns
Drafting an Investment Policy Statement	Investment Policy Statement?
A well-diversified portfolio	A non-diversified portfolio to magnify the results of security selection
Balancing tax implications with investment decision-making	Not balancing tax implications with investment decision-making
Simple and easy to understand investments	Chasing the latest investment fads
Realistic, achievable and measurable goals	Unrealistic, unachievable and immeasurable goals
Empirical research	Unproven methods

This book examines Optimal Investing from the perspective of asset allocation. Asset allocation is not a new theory, but it is somewhat complex and often times misunderstood. This book will present asset allocation in a way easily understood by both the novice and intermediate investor.

My sole focus is to present the material in a framework that is more like a step-by-step how to guide, rather than a textbook filled with technical jargon written primarily for investment advisors and those with advanced knowledge of asset allocation. As you will see, the book will begin with an overview of asset allocation and then discuss how to apply asset allocation theory to designing, constructing, monitoring, and rebalancing your investment portfolio. Lastly, I will mention some important considerations that investors should know and possibly take action on.

I wrote Optimal Investing based on the following guiding principles:

- You want to feel secure and in control of your investment portfolio.
- You want to protect your investment portfolio from large swings in market value.
- You want to achieve both your pre-retirement and retirement financial goals.
- You want to be knowledgeable on the subject of asset allocation.
- You want to read more of a step-by-step how to guide than to read a textbook full of technical jargon.
- You want to learn what not to do as much as you want to learn what to do.

To better understand asset allocation, I sometimes use football as an analogy. For example, each football team involves an owner, head coach and players. Likewise, asset allocation involves a portfolio owner, portfolio manager (which could be you), and asset classes. Football is comprised of a certain number of players, while asset allocation is comprised of a certain number of asset classes. Football players are differentiated by their abilities and so to are asset classes. In football, there is a time for offense and a time for defense. So to can be said for asset allocation, simply think of bull and bear markets. To be successful in football, players must work together as a team. Likewise, to be successful with your investment portfolio, your asset mix must work together as a team. No team will win with all individuals.

Lastly, I often comment how asset allocation is similar to wearing protective football equipment; helmets, shoulder pads, kneepads, etc. If you were to take off your equipment, you could probably run faster, cut easier and catch the ball easier. As a result, you would probably score more touchdowns. However, it doesn't take a rocket scientist to recognize that not wearing the protective equipment is not at all practical. One hit from your opponent and you could be out of the game for a very long time, if not forever.

Phases of the Portfolio Management Process

Portfolio management has four distinct phases. These phases include designing, constructing, monitoring, and rebalancing.

FIGURE I.1

Four Phases of Portfolio Management

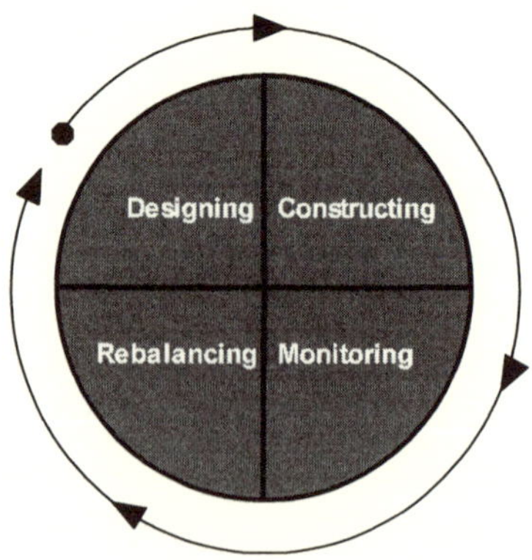

Asset allocation theory is applied to your investment portfolio in all four phases of the portfolio management process. In the chapter on designing your optimal portfolio you will learn how to establish your optimal asset mix, or the asset classes and asset subclasses that will give you the highest expected total rate of return for the level of risk you are willing and able to assume. The discussion on constructing your optimal portfolio involves how best to implement the plan you created in the design phase. The chapter on monitoring will show you how to evaluate your portfolio in regards to performance measurement and appropriateness of your asset mix given changes over time. Lastly, in the chapter on rebalancing, you will learn how to properly adjust and reallocate your asset mix in order to retain the optimal portfolio.

Each one of the four phases, including "how to" steps and the biggest mistakes investors make will be discussed in detail in part two of this book.

In the first chapter we will discuss what drives investment performance. In chapters two through four we will discuss the foundation of asset allocation and explain both asset classes and asset allocation strategies. Although some of this information may not be new to you, it will be new to others. As a result, I will discuss the basics at the outset to ensure readers are comfortable with the material. Afterwards, we will discuss how best to apply asset allocation to build your optimal portfolio.

Part 1

Overview of Asset Allocation

Chapter 1

Determinants of Investment Performance

♦ ♦ ♦

I would rather be certain of a good return than hopeful of a great one.

– Warren Buffett

What Drives Investment Performance?

It is no secret that the majority of portfolio managers do not beat the return of the market each year. Furthermore, those portfolio managers who do beat the market in any given year have a lower probability of beating the market in the following year. Why? Is it poor market timing? Is it careless stock picking? Is it simply the result of bad luck? No. The principal reason the majority of portfolio managers do not beat the return of the market in any given year is because they failed to create, apply and emphasize a sound asset allocation policy to the management of investment portfolios.

Empirical Research

In 1986, a landmark study entitled "Determinants of Portfolio Performance" published in the *Financial Analysts Journal* (July-August 1986, pp. 39-44), authors Gary P. Brinson, L. Randolph Hood, and Gilbert L. Beebower concluded that asset allocation policy is by far the principle determinant of investment performance. Contrary to popular belief at the time, the researchers found that security selection and market timing determine only a small fraction of investment performance.

FIGURE 1.1

Determinants of Investment Performance

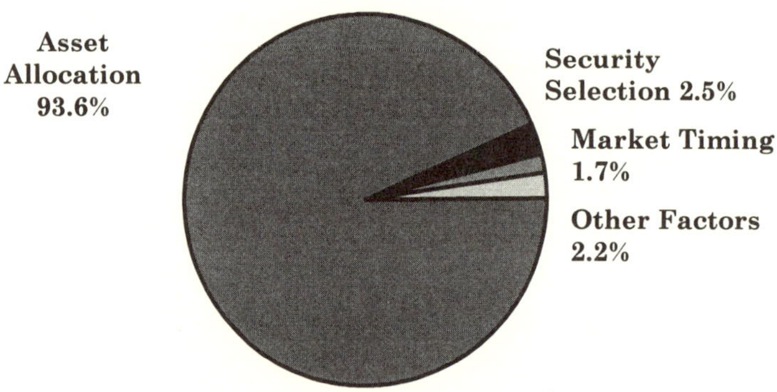

Source: "Determinants of Portfolio Performance" by Gary P. Brinson, L. Randolph Hood, and Gilbert L. Beebower, *Financial Analysts Journal*, July - August 1986.

Asset Allocation

The strategy of dividing an investor's wealth among the different asset classes and asset subclasses to achieve the highest expected total rate of return.

Security Selection

The strategy of determining which investments to buy or sell for a portfolio. Commonly referred to as stock picking.

Market Timing

The strategy of determining when to purchase or sell an investment.

Security

An investable asset, excluding insurance policies, fixed annuities, and futures contracts, which can be purchased and sold.

The aforementioned study was based on the quarterly investment results of ninety large pension funds over a ten-year period from 1974 to 1983. The goal of the study was to determine to what degree asset allocation policy, security selection, market timing, and to a lesser extent, costs contributed to the investment performance of the pension funds under study.

Asset allocation policy was analyzed within the context of three primary asset classes: stocks, bonds, and cash. For example, one pension fund might have an asset mix of 65% stocks, 25% bonds, and 10% cash while another pension fund might have an asset mix of 50% stocks, 35% bonds, and 15% cash. Market timing was evaluated by analyzing the changes in asset class weightings over time. For instance, if a portfolio manager altered a pension fund's allocation to the three observed asset classes over a given time period, the researchers interpreted that as an attempt by the portfolio manager to profit from market timing. As you can see from Figure 1.1, asset allocation policy explained 93.6% of investment performance while security selection, market timing, and other factors (including costs) explained 2.5%, 1.7% and 2.2% of investment performance, respectively.

In 1991, a follow-up study by Gary P. Brinson, Gilbert L. Beebower, and Brian D. Singer entitled "Determinants of Portfolio Performance II: An Update" published in the *Financial Analysts Journal* (May-June 1991, pp 40-48) was made using updated information. This study arrived at nearly the same conclusion as the previous study. As such, the subsequent study concluded that asset allocation policy is the primary factor explaining investment performance over time. Again, the second study found that security selection and market timing explained only a fraction of investment performance.

FIGURE 1.2

Determinants of Investment Performance

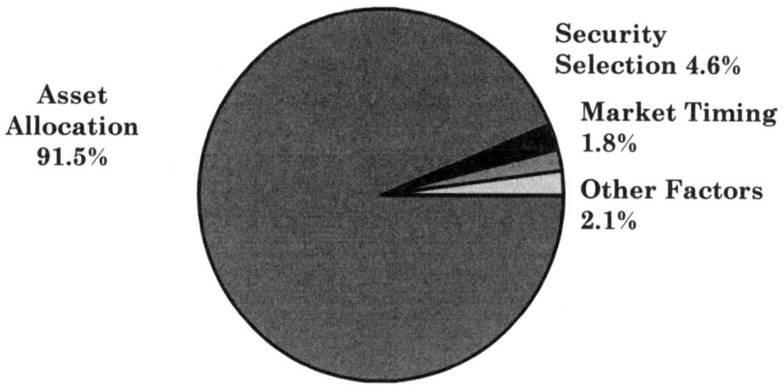

Source: "Determinants of Portfolio Performance II: An Update" by Gary P. Brinson, Gilbert L. Beebower and Brian D. Singer, *Financial Analysts Journal*, May – June 1991.

As you can see from Figure 1.2, asset allocation policy was found to explain 91.5% of investment performance while security selection, market timing and other factors explained 4.6%, 1.8% and 2.1% of investment performance, respectively.

In yet another significant research study, renowned practitioners Roger G. Ibbotson and Paul D. Kaplan in early 2000 concluded in their study entitled "Does Asset Allocation Policy Explain 40, 90, or 100 Percent of Performance" published in the *Financial Analysts Journal* (January-February 2000, pp. 26-33) that asset allocation policy explains about 90% of investment performance over time. A copy of this study can be obtained from the Ibbotson Associates company web page at www.Ibbotson.com.

If security selection and market timing do not play a significant role in determining investment performance over time, a good question to investigate is whether or not individual industries play a role. According to Eugene F. Fama and Kenneth R. French they generally do not. In their research entitled "Industry Costs of Equity" published in the *Journal of Financial Economics,* 1997, the researchers concluded that although specific industries can influence market prices, they do so only in a random and short-term way. I'm not sure about you, but I'm not willing to invest in a short-term way in my retirement portfolio.

For a real world example, all you have to do is to look at the numerous financial magazines touting the best mutual funds to invest in for the upcoming year. Have you ever noticed how the majority of mutual funds that made these lists were not on the lists from the previous year or even the previous 5 years? Wait until next year and see which mutual funds make the best mutual funds lists. I bet you will discover very few that repeat. Regardless of whether or not these financial magazines are right on with their picks, it clearly demonstrates how portfolio managers cannot beat the market consistently. If they could, then wouldn't there be more mutual funds repeating on the best to invest in lists?

I have probably purchased fifty 'hot tips' in my career, maybe even more. When I put them all together, I know I am a net loser.

– Charles Schwab

To be fair to those who are strong proponents of emphasizing security selection over asset allocation, there have been some research studies concluding that, although asset allocation does determine a significant amount of investment performance, it does not determine to the extent of the aforementioned research studies. With that being said, should we downplay or even disregard studies concluding that asset allocation determines a lesser part of investment performance? No, but I think we need to take it into consideration when making investment decisions. Focusing entirely on security selection or market timing is similar to throwing a Hail Mary pass on every play in football. Rather, investing is about gaining yardage successfully and consistently. The message here is that asset allocation does determine a significant portion of your investment performance over time.

Contrary to what impression I may have given you I am not anti-security selection. Empirical evidence has concluded that it does explain a portion of investment performance over time. As a result, I believe security selection does have a place within the portfolio management process. However, you need to focus your time and resources on that strategy, namely asset allocation, where you can have a meaningful impact on your investment performance. Impacting your investment performance via security selection or market timing is much more difficult than via asset allocation. You should emphasize asset allocation first, and then move to security selection or market timing if you so desire.

If I have noticed anything over these 60 years on Wall Street, it is that people do not succeed in forecasting what's going to happen to the stock market.

– Benjamin Graham

Chapter 2

Fundamentals of Asset Allocation

♦ ♦ ♦

Foundation of Asset Allocation Theory

Asset allocation is founded on two celebrated and highly influential investment theories. The two include the modern portfolio theory (MPT) and the efficient market hypothesis (EMH), which is essentially a refinement of MPT. Modern portfolio theory says that investors and portfolio managers should not evaluate each security on a stand-alone basis. Rather, each security should be evaluated based on its ability to enhance the overall risk and return trade-off profile of the portfolio. In addition, modern portfolio theory says that when an investor is faced with two investments with identical expected returns but different levels of risk, he or she should select the investment that has the lower risk. Said another way, a rational investor will select the investment with the higher return when faced with two investments that have different expected returns but identical levels of risk. This type of investor is termed the risk adverse investor.

FIGURE 2.1

Investment Alternatives and Rational Decisions

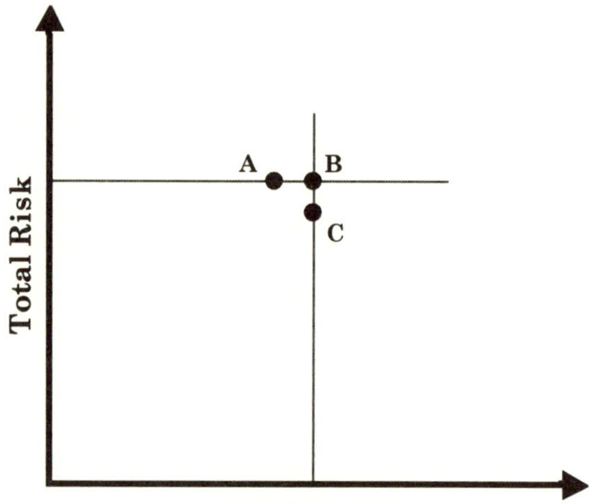

When faced with investments A & B, a rational investor will select investment B over investment A because the total return of investment B is higher, with both having the same level of risk. Moreover, when faced with investments B & C, a rational investor will select investment C over investment B because the total risk of investment C is lower, with both having the same total return.

Lastly, modern portfolio theory introduces the concept of correlation and stresses how it enhances the risk and return trade-off profile of a portfolio. The Employee Retirement Income Security Act of 1974, which governs the management of pension funds, emphasizes this point, thus essentially endorsing MPT. Harry M. Markowitz, who was awarded the Noble Prize in

Economics in 1990, is considered the "father of modern portfolio theory" for this work.

The efficient market hypothesis, a term coined by Eugene F. Fama, says that security prices are fair and reasonable because they fully reflect all available public and non-public information that might impact them. As a result, security selection and market timing are said to fail over the long-term since every investor has the same information. Therefore, it is the amounts of risk investors accept that explain their investment performance over time. Contrary to misconception, the EMH does not conclude that investors can't beat the market. Over any holding period there will be some investors who beat the market, but most will not. The number of investors who beat the market will be no greater than expected by standard mathematical probability. Statistical outliers are common. It is simply the law of large numbers.

For argument sake, let's say the market is not completely efficient and therefore sizeable opportunities do exist to beat the market consistently. This assumption raises an important question. Do individual investors have the means and ability to take advantage of these opportunities? Unfortunately the chances of doing so are rather small. Given our increasingly competitive investment environment and accelerating developments in information technology, undervalued securities only exist for very short periods. With the vast number of highly skilled investment professionals, these undervalued securities disappear quickly. What does this mean in practice to you and me? It means:

- The financial markets are exceedingly efficient
- No investor can earn highly excessive investment returns consistently
- That risk and return are invariably linked

I believe in efficient markets. I know nothing about stock picking. I don't trust anyone else to interpret the data better than myself so I don't believe the opportunities are there to beat the market.

– Eugene F. Fama

Asset Allocation Theory

As mentioned in the previous chapter, asset allocation is the principal determinant of investment performance over time. A proper asset allocation policy will not only achieve your specific financial goals, but also will protect your portfolio from serious market corrections. The singular aim of asset allocation is to maximize a portfolio's expected total rate of return for the level of risk an investor is willing and able to assume. As crazy as it may sound, you will increase your investment return without increasing risk with the proper asset allocation policy. Employing the proper asset allocation policy leads to building an optimal portfolio, the goal every rational investor should have.

In addition to maximizing your expected return for the given level of risk you assume, asset allocation also reduces the volatility within your portfolio. The more asset classes and asset subclasses you employ the less portfolio volatility you will experience. Each asset class performs differently at different times. Thus, during any one period, one asset class may perform well, while another may not.

As with most everything, one size does not fit all with asset allocation. Depending on your unique circumstances and preferences, you can customize your portfolio by allocating more or less to each asset class. Consequently, if you desire more return and are willing to accept more risk, you can allocate more to higher risk asset classes. Conversely, if you wish to accept less risk, you have the option to allocate more of your assets to lower risk asset classes.

Optimal Asset Allocation Policy

Determining which asset classes to invest in and in what proportion is based exclusively on your investment objectives and constraints.

Objectives
The return aspiration, such as protecting capital or receiving current income, and risk tolerance desired by an investor.

Constraints
Parameters and limitations that must be adhered to when designing, constructing, monitoring and rebalancing a portfolio.

In practice, portfolio managers focus on two objectives; return aspiration and risk tolerance. Likewise, portfolio managers focus on five constraints; time horizon, liquidity needs, tax considerations, legal and regulatory considerations, and unique circumstances and preferences.

Objectives:

Return Aspiration
The financial reward sought by an investor for investing the assets of the portfolio.

Risk Tolerance
The degree of risk an investor is willing and able to assume to make an investment.

Constraints

Time Horizon
The length of time an investor plans to invest the assets of the portfolio. Also referred to as time period or holding period.

Liquidity Needs

The degree to which an investor requires cash and its equivalents to support everyday activities and special purchases.

Tax Considerations

The attention that is given to realizing, deferring or avoiding taxes. For example, the tax on current income and the tax on capital gains must be balanced. Other taxes include estate and trust taxes.

Legal & Regulatory Considerations

Laws and regulations an investor and portfolio manager are obligated to follow. For instance, trust administration, prudent expert rule, and IRA contributions and withdrawals.

Unique Circumstances & Preferences

This constraint essentially incorporates anything that cannot be categorized in one of the other four constraints. Examples include unusual preferences of the investor that impairs in some way the portfolio management process or an investor's financial support for a dependent parent.

But what are objectives and constraints based on? Objectives and constraints are based on your needs, such as:

- Establishing an emergency fund
- Buying a home
- Entertaining
- Paying for private schooling
- Saving for a child's college education
- Starting a business
- Buying a vacation home
- Joining a country club
- Donating money to charity

Over time your needs, and therefore your objectives and constraints, will change. Thus, your stage in life will have a significant impact on the investment process. There are four primary lifecycle phases people live through:

FIGURE 2.2

Lifecycle Phases [1]

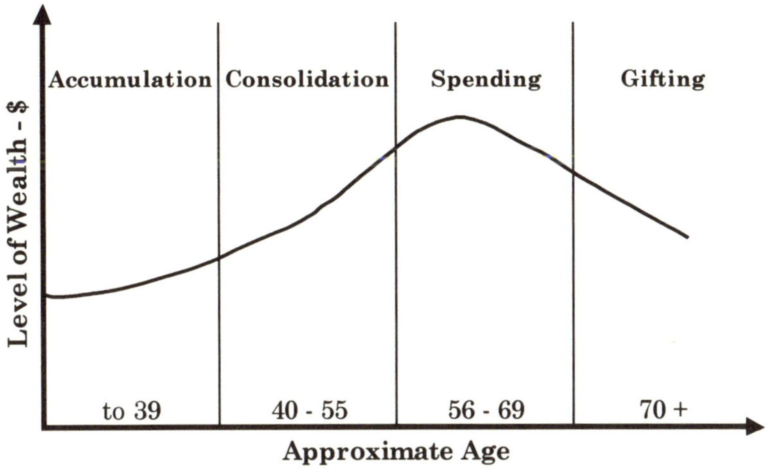

[1] Adapted from Frank K. Reilly and Keith C. Brown, *Investment Analysis and Portfolio Management*, 5th edition, The Dryden Press, 1997

Although not always the case, people in each lifecycle phase tend to share similar needs and goals. As you can see from Figure 2.2, the underlying determinant of each lifecycle phase is the level of wealth. As people accumulate more wealth over time, their needs and goals naturally change.

People in the Accumulation Lifecycle Phase:

Profile: Typically people in their early careers with long-term time horizons. Their wealth, and sometimes their income, is small relative to their debt and expenses.

Common Goals:

Short-term To buy a house and other essential assets.

Long-term To start a college education fund and begin saving for retirement.

People in the Consolidation Lifecycle Phase:

Profile: Typically people in their middle to late working years when their time horizons are still relatively long. As they progress through this phase their income begins to exceed their expenses.

Common Goals:

Short-term To increase their standard of living and increase their free time.

Long-term To significantly add to their retirement savings.

People in the Spending Lifecycle Phase:

Profile: Typically people in their late careers to early retirement when their time horizons can be anywhere from 7 to 20+ years, thus moderate to long-term time horizons. Their expenses often exceed their income, which is sometimes supplemented by investment and retirement income.

Common Goals:

Short-term To maintain their standard of living.

Long-term To protect their wealth.

People in the Gifting Lifecycle Phase:

Profile: Typically people well into their retirement years with declining investment time horizons. In this phase an individual owns more assets than he or she will ever need. To supplement retirement, assets are sometimes sold.

Common Goals:

Short-term To maintain their health and well-being.

Long-term To distribute their wealth to family members and philanthropic organizations.

Since objectives and constraints differ from investor to investor depending on either their lifecycle phase or individual preferences, so to will their allocations to different asset classes.

Who is Asset Allocation Appropriate For?

Asset allocation is a critical yet simple concept that should be applied to nearly all types of portfolios. Individual accounts, endowments, foundations, pension plans, 401(k)s, businesses, and other accounts can benefit greatly from its application. Most institutions have been utilizing an asset allocation methodology in their investment planning and management process for some time while its use and application by individual investors is beginning to grow strongly.

Return and Risk

Two of the most important concepts an investor should learn and fully understand are return and risk. These two concepts and how they work together are the foundations of asset allocation theory and its application to building an optimal portfolio. Depending on your objectives and constraints, you may invest in assets which exhibit low risk and therefore the potential for low, but stable returns, or you may invest in assets which exhibit high risk and therefore the potential for high, but often times, volatile returns. In basic asset allocation theory, the higher the potential risk you take, the higher the potential return you should earn. Rational investors will not assume a higher risk for the same potential return that a lower risk asset offers.

Return

The return of an investment is of primary importance to you and other investors. Without expectations of appropriate compensation in the form of returns, people would not invest their hard earned money. Although we will be discussing quantitative measures of return, do not forget that return often has qualitative rewards. Qualitative rewards include security, simplicity, and control for instance.

Return

The profit or loss, usually expressed in percentage terms, an investor receives for making an investment for a specific period of time, often called the holding period.

The profit or loss from an investment is comprised of:

- Appreciation or depreciation of the market value of a security during the holding period
- Dividends or interest received from a security during the holding period

Summing the above two profit or loss components and dividing by the market value of the investment at the beginning of the period will give what is referred to as total return. This measure takes into account both the change in price of the security and any cash flow received during the holding period. It is commonplace in the investment field to measure return using the total return calculation. An example of calculating total return is as follows:

Example: The Jones Foundation purchased 1,000 shares of Deere & Co at \$40 a share. One year later the Jones Foundation sold the investment for \$44 a share. During the one-year period, Deere & Co paid a \$1 per share dividend. The total return of the investment, not including transaction costs, is as follows:

$$\frac{\$4 \text{ (appreciation)} + \$1 \text{ (dividend)}}{\$40 \text{ (cost)}} = 12\tfrac{1}{2}\%$$

Thus, to calculate total return, one must sum the appreciation (ending value less the beginning value) and all interest and dividends received during the period and divide by the beginning value.

Even small differences in your rate of return can have big results. The following chart illustrates how small differences in rates of return can make large differences in the value of an investment over time.

FIGURE 2.3

How Rates of Return and Time Impact the Growth of a $10,000 Investment

Holding	Value at the End of the Holding Period				
Period (Years)	3%	6%	9%	12%	15%
5	$11,593	$13,382	$15,386	$17,623	$20,114
10	$13,439	$17,908	$23,674	$31,058	$40,456
20	$18,061	$32,071	$56,044	$96,463	$163,665
30	$24,273	$57,435	$132,677	$299,599	$662,118
50	$43,839	$184,202	$743,575	$2,890,022	$10,836,574

Source: Frush Financial Group

The concept of return can be divided into two distinctions, actual return and expected return. Actual return is the return you have realized, or one that has occurred in a past holding period. Conversely, expected return is an estimate of what you will earn, both appreciation and income (dividends and interest), in a future holding period. Both actual and expected returns are commonly expressed as annualized percentages. The process of forecasting expected returns is especially difficult. However, the following basic steps will provide you with a cursory understanding:

1. Forecast all possible material outcomes that may occur
2. Assign probabilities of occurrence to each outcome
3. Forecast the results for each specific material outcome
4. Multiply the possible outcomes with the appropriate resulting return and then add the results for each possible outcome

Example: An analyst estimates that the Smith Company has a 50% probability of returning 12%, 25% probability of returning 5%, 15% probability of returning 0% and a 10% probability of returning –5%:

$$(.50 \times .12) + (.25 \times .05) + (.15 \times 0) + (.10 \times (-.05)) = 6.75\%$$

Potential outcomes are usually based on estimates of how well the economy will perform in the future holding period. The resulting return is simply an estimate given each economic scenario.

Risk

There are different ways investors define risk. Some investors define risk as losing money, while others define risk as unfamiliar investments. Still others define risk as contrarian risk, or the risk investors feel when they are not "following the crowd". If you were to toss out all of the subjective definitions, risk is defined more objectively as uncertainty, or the uncertainty that actual investment returns will equal expected returns.

Since you rely on estimates of future returns to design your optimal portfolio, it is critically important that actual returns match expected returns. The greater the predictability of an investment's return, the lower risk the investment is said to have. Conversely, the less predictable an investment's return, the higher risk an investment is said to have.

Risk

Uncertainty. Specifically, the uncertainty that an investment's actual return will match its expected return.

Different investments possess different types and different amounts of risk, and therefore different expected returns. Each type of risk is derived from one or more sources of risk.

What are the sources of risk?

There are two primary sources of risk. The first is called systematic risk, or risk attributed to relatively uncontrollable external factors. The second is called unsystematic risk, or risk attributed directly to the underlying investment.

Systematic Risk

Systematic risk results from conditions, events and trends occurring outside the scope of the investment. The four principle types of systematic risk include the following:

- **Exchange Rate Risk:** The risk that an investment's value will be impacted by changes in the foreign currency market. For example, if your U.S. currency must be converted into a foreign currency to purchase a foreign investment, then changes in the value of that foreign currency relative to the U.S. dollar will impact your return.
- **Interest Rate Risk:** The risk attributed to the loss in market value due to an increase in the general level of interest rates. Why do market values decline when interest rates rise? Primarily because as interest rates increase the availability of more attractive investments with higher yields also increases.
- **Market Risk:** The risk attributed to the loss in market value due to the declining movement of the entire market portfolio.
- **Purchasing Power Risk:** The risk attributed to inflation and how it erodes the real value of an investment over time.

FIGURE 2.4

Impact of Inflation on the Value of $100 Over Time

Holding Period (Years)	Value at the End of the Holding Period 2%	3%	5%	7%	9%
5	$ 90	$ 86	$ 77	$ 70	$ 62
10	$ 82	$ 74	$ 60	$ 48	$ 39
20	$ 67	$ 54	$ 36	$ 23	$ 15
30	$ 55	$ 40	$ 21	$ 11	$ 6
50	$ 36	$ 22	$ 8	$ 3	$ 1

Source: Frush Financial Group

At any one point, there are different degrees of each risk occurring. These risks will cause the demand for a particular investment to rise or fall, thus impacting actual returns.

Unsystematic Risk

Unlike systematic risk, unsystematic risk does not come from external factors. This source of risk is unique to an investment, such as how much debt a company possesses, what actions a company's management takes and what industry it operates in. The principle types of unsystematic risk include:

- **Business Risk:** The risk attributed to a company's operations, particularly those involving sales and income.
- **Financial Risk:** The risk attributed to a company's financial stability and structure, namely the company's use of debt to leverage earnings. The greater use of debt the more risky a company is.

Creditors have better memories than debtors.

– Benjamin Franklin

- **Industry Risk:** The risk attributed to a group of companies within a particular industry due to events within that group that impacts everyone.
- **Liquidity Risk:** The risk that an investment cannot be executed in the secondary market at or near market prices.
- **Call Risk:** The risk attributed to an event where a security may be called prior to maturity leaving the investor unable to reinvest the proceeds at the same or a higher rate of return. This risk is associated with bonds and preferred stock.
- **Regulation Risk:** The risk that new laws and regulations will negatively impact the market value of an investment. For example, a state government may pass a law requiring manufacturers to add new and costly pollution control systems in their factories.

Summing systematic and unsystematic risk equals total risk. Since the goal of asset allocation is to create a well-diversified portfolio, unsystematic risk is considered unimportant because it should be essentially eliminated. Therefore, an optimal portfolio should only possess systematic risk, or risk resulting from market and uncontrollable external factors.

How to measure risk

Since different investments have both different types of risk and different degrees of risk, it is essential that we are able to quantify risk to make comparisons across the broad range of asset classes. As mentioned earlier, risk can be defined as the uncertainty that an investment's actual return will match its expected return. Intuitively one can see that the greater the difference between actual and expected returns equals the less predictable and uncertain the investment is. This situation translates to greater risk. Using historical return data, we are able to define risk more accurately. In simple analysis, averaging the degrees of difference between actual and expected returns for a given investment gives us the statistical measure termed standard deviation. A higher standard deviation translates into higher risk.

Standard Deviation

A statistical measure of the degree to which actual returns are spread around the mean actual return. Expressed as a percentage, standard deviation is considered the best measure of risk.

Since an investment's actual returns are impacted by both systematic and unsystematic risks, standard deviation is a measure of an investment's total risk. Although standard deviation is one of the best measures of risk, it is by far not without issues. Depending on the holding periods selected for comparison, standard deviation may vary from analysis to analysis. Due to many factors, it is best to utilize a standard deviation that is derived from actual returns from the last 10 to 20 years. Utilizing returns older than 20 years may incorporate risks in the investment which are no longer present or were not present over 20 years ago. For example, 30 years ago tobacco companies were not inundated with class-action lawsuits regarding the health concerns of smoking. Today these class-action lawsuits can have a significant impact on their stock prices. Consequently, using data collected from recent periods is more appropriate to calculate standard deviation.

Beta

A measure of risk. The degree of security price volatility in relation to the overall market. Expressed as an absolute number rather than as a percentage.

Another measure of risk in common use is called beta. This measure is easier to understand, calculate and apply than standard deviation, but it too has drawbacks. The most significant is that beta is not representative of total risk. Beta is derived from the volatility of a given investment relative to the overall market. Thus, beta only measures systematic, or market risk, and not unsystematic risk. Remember, however, that a properly built portfolio will have minimal unsystematic risk since it should be diversified away.

Beta is expressed in absolute rather than percentage terms. A beta of above 1 is considered more volatile than the market, whereas a beta of less than 1 is considered less volatile than the overall market. Lastly, betas of 1 move in sync with the overall market. Thus, if an investment has a beta of 1.5 then that investment will be 50% more volatile than the overall market while an investment with a beta of .75 will be 25% less volatile than the overall market.

Example: Stock A has a beta of 1.2. Thus, if the S&P 500 is expected to rise by 5% during the holding period, then Stock A is expected to rise by 6% (5% multiplied by 1.2). Conversely, if the S&P 500 is expected to fall by 5% during the holding period, then Stock A is expected to fall by 6%.

As you can see from the above example, when the market is rising higher beta investments generally earn higher returns than the overall market. Conversely, when the market is declining, these same investments generally have lower returns than the overall market.

In practice, investors desiring market rates of return can generally obtain them by investing in securities with betas of 1. Moreover, investors desiring to be more aggressive can potentially obtain higher returns by investing in securities with betas higher than 1. Of course, securities with betas above 1 have more inherent risk.

The charts on the following pages illustrate why volatility is used as a measure of risk. Figure 2.5 presents two securities with the same 10% expected return per year, but with different degrees of volatility - security A has a low degree of price volatility while security B has a high degree of price volatility.

FIGURE 2.5

Volatility as a Risk Measure I

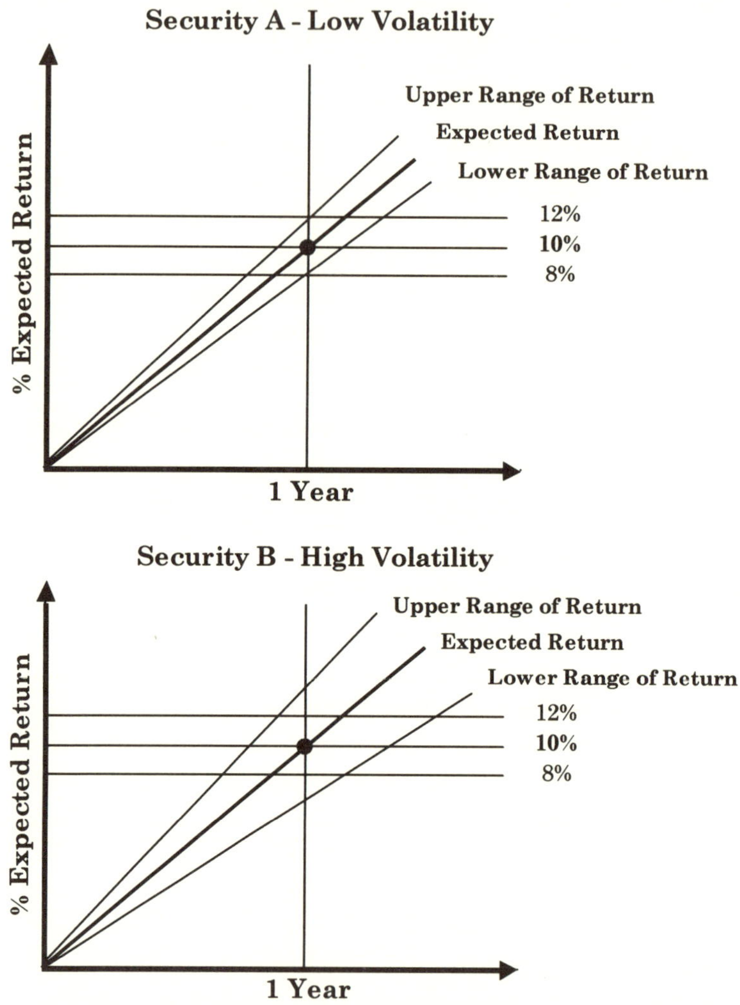

As you can see from Figure 2.5, although security A does not have the upside potential as does security B, security A does not posses the downside potential as well. Remember, investing is not about swinging for homeruns on every pitch. Moreover, if you desire a higher expected return, simply investment in a security with a higher expected return.

Figure 2.6 presents volatility as a risk measure in a slightly different way. In this figure we use the same securities, A and B (from Figure 2.5), but this time we want to determine which security has the greater probability of earning a return of at least 9%.

FIGURE 2.6

Volatility as a Risk Measure II

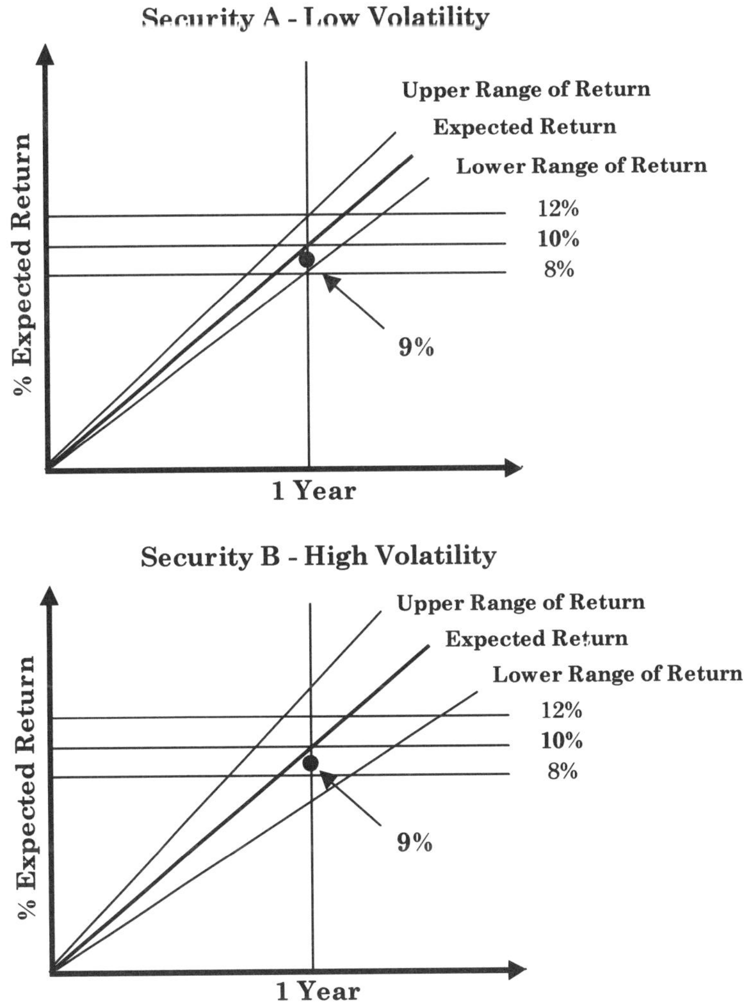

If we were to assign expected return ranges of 8 – 12% for security A and 6 – 14% for security B, then security A will have the higher probability of earning at least a 9% return one year later. As mentioned previously, a security with a higher probability, or less uncertainty, of achieving a certain expected return is considered less risky. For those of you more quantitative, below is the basic math on how to calculate the probability. For simplicity, the example does not take into consideration the concept of the bell curve:

$$\textbf{Security A} = 100\% - \left(\frac{9\% - 8\%}{12\% - 8\%} \right) = 75\% \text{ probability}$$

$$\textbf{Security B} = 100\% - \left(\frac{9\% - 6\%}{14\% - 6\%} \right) = 63\% \text{ probability}$$

FIGURE 2.7

Historical Volatility from 1941 to 2002

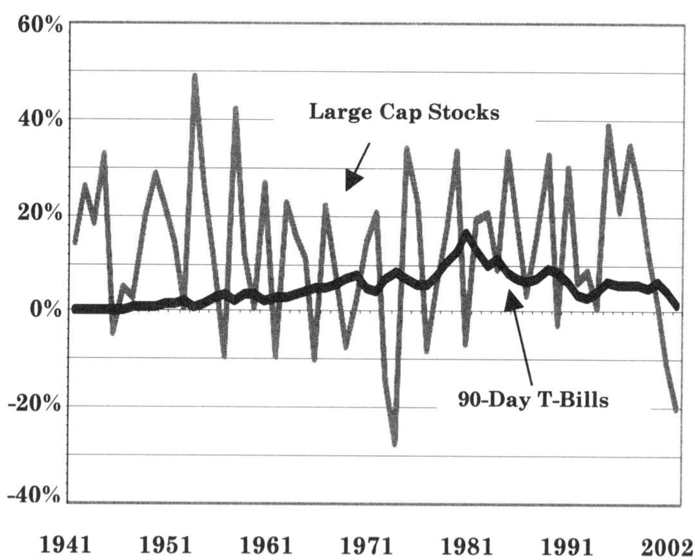

Source: Center for Research in Security Prices at the University of Chicago.

Risk & Return Relationship

In principle, investors who take greater risk should be compensated with greater return. Depending on your risk tolerance, the more risk you assume the higher the expected return. To better understand this relationship between risk and expected return, a model called the efficient frontier was developed. The efficient frontier plots different investments on an upward sloping curved line according to their risk and return trade-off profile.

Efficient Frontier

All possible optimal portfolio combinations where the expected total rate of return is maximized given the specific level of risk assumed. Usually illustrated as a curved line within the risk-return graph.

As you can see from Figure 2.8, by moving up the efficient frontier, investments present the potential for greater return, but also greater risk. Nevertheless, each point on the efficient frontier exhibits the highest expected total rate of return for the level of risk present.

Your objective is to select investments somewhere along the efficient frontier within the context of your objectives and constraints. Some investors will place their investments toward the top of the slope while others with lower risk tolerances will place their investments on a lower part of the slope. An investor approaching retirement, for example, will begin moving down the slope while a person approaching their peak earning years may move up the slope as their tolerance for risk becomes greater.

Regardless of whether your portfolio is comprised of 50% equities and 50% fixed-income or 40% equities, 40% fixed-income and 20% cash and equivalents, as long as each portfolio combination exhibits the highest expected total rate of return it will be plotted somewhere along the efficient frontier. Portfolios that do not exhibit the highest expected total rates of return will be plotted below the slope of the efficient frontier.

FIGURE 2.8

Hypothetical Efficient Frontier

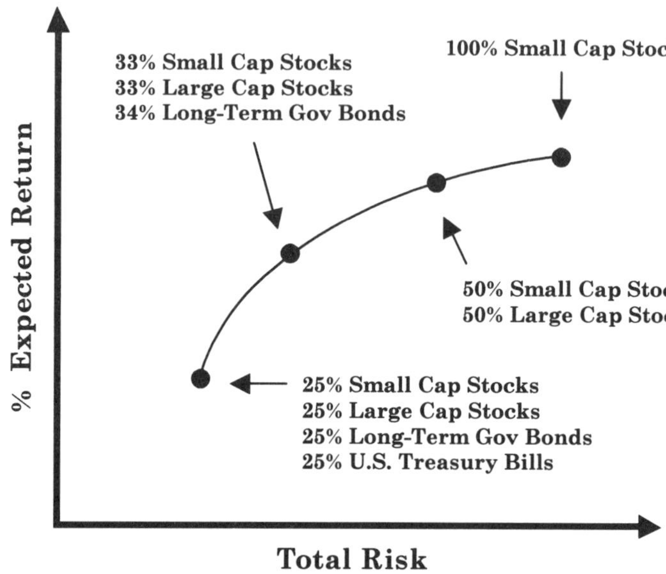

Understanding the relationship between risk and return is critical as it underlies the process of allocating assets. Without a true understanding of this relationship, you may design a portfolio with either greater risk than desired or experience actual returns that do not meet objectives due to designing your portfolio with less risky assets. As we will see in the next few chapters, the process of asset allocation involves estimating expected returns for each asset class and then determining, within the context of your objectives and constraints, what percentage of the portfolio should be allocated to each asset class.

Risk and return trade-off profile

Given the direct relationship between risk and return, we are able to measure this relationship and use that measurement to build a portfolio with the appropriate risk and return trade-off profile. By using what is called the Sharpe Ratio, or simply dividing the excess expected return of an asset class by its standard deviation (level of risk), we are able to ascertain the amount of excess expected return per unit of risk for an asset class. Doing so helps us to compare, contrast and select asset classes with dissimilar excess expected returns and risk levels. Excess expected return is the expected return minus the risk-free rate, or the rate one can earn from investing in U.S. treasury bills.

Example: Suppose we have two asset classes, A & B. Asset class A has a standard deviation of 6% and an excess expected return of 8% over the proposed holding period. By dividing the excess expected return of 8% by the standard deviation of 6%, we find that asset class A has a risk and return trade-off profile of 1.33. Asset class B has a standard deviation of 4% and an excess expected return of 6%. This translates into a risk and return trade-off profile of 1.5. As you can see, although asset class A has the higher expected return, it clearly does not provide the highest level of expected return per unit of risk. Asset class B does in this example.

Sharpe Ratio

A method developed by William F. Sharpe to measure the risk-adjusted return of an investment or portfolio. This method calculates the amount of excess return per unit of risk.

Correlation Among Asset Classes

An optimal portfolio is not just the sum of its parts. Rather, an optimal portfolio is the sum of its synergies. Synergies are created by the interaction of the asset classes held within a portfolio. This interaction is commonly referred to as correlation and is a critical input to the asset allocation process.

Correlation

The technical term used to measure how closely the prices of two investments move together over time.

Positively correlated assets move in the same direction, both up and down. Conversely, negatively correlated assets move in opposite directions. Correlations between two assets are expressed on a scale between –1 and +1. The more two assets are correlated, or tend to move together, the closer to +1. Similarly, the more two assets tend to move in opposite directions, the closer to –1. A measure of +1 means that both assets move exactly together while a measure if –1 means that both assets move exactly opposite of each other. Note, a measure of 0 means the two asset classes move entirely independent of each other, thus no correlation of any kind.

Example: The correlation between Stock A and Stock B is .8. As a result, for every $1 price movement in either stock, the other will move 80% in the same direction in any given period.

Should you seek out asset classes that have higher or lower correlations? By investing in asset classes which posses low to negative correlations, you are able to reduce total portfolio risk without impacting the return of your portfolio. Doing so will help to greatly minimize overall risk resulting from each asset class' inherent systematic risk.

In theory, you should therefore only invest in asset classes that are perfectly negatively correlated. However, in the real world there are no asset classes which are perfectly negatively correlated, or a –1. In reality most, but not all, asset classes are positively correlated to some degree. Given the existence of no perfectly negative correlations between asset classes, you should focus on those asset classes that are less than perfectly positively correlated, thus receiving some benefits of asset correlation.

FIGURE 2.9

Correlation of Annual Returns from December 31, 1925 – December 31, 2002

	Large Cap Stocks	Small Cap Stocks	U.S. Treasury Bills	Long-Term U.S. Gov Bonds	Inflation (CPI)
Large Cap Stocks	1.00	0.87	0.02	0.13	*
Small Cap Stocks		1.00	-0.01	0.09	*
U.S. Treasury Bills			1.00	0.23	0.24
Long-Term U.S. Gov Bonds				1.00	-0.02
Inflation (CPI)					1.00

* Slightly negative - close to zero

Source: Calculated by the Frush Financial Group based on data supplied by the Center for Research in Security Prices at the University of Chicago.

Diversification

It is very important to understand that diversification is not the same as asset allocation. Asset allocation involves investing in those asset classes which posses a risk and return trade-off profile that will achieve your objectives and constraints. On the other hand, diversification involves investing in a significant number of securities within each asset class in order to minimize company-specific risk. Diversification only minimizes risk, while asset allocation maximizes return for the level of risk you are willing and able to assume.

Is it possible to have a diversified portfolio without having an optimal portfolio? Unfortunately it is possible. I liken this to a sort of investment anomaly. If your portfolio were only allocated to equity securities but owned an appropriate number of them, then the portfolio could be considered diversified. If your objectives and constraints called for investing only 60% of your assets in equities and the remaining assets in fixed-income and cash & equivalents, then the same portfolio would not be considered optimal. To be considered optimal, a portfolio's expected total rate of return must be the highest possible given the level of risk you are willing and able to assume. Diversification does not involve maximizing returns, only minimizing risk. With that being said, it is important to point out that asset allocation is dependent on diversification. Minimizing risk is underscored by the concept of diversification. Moreover, diversification is essential to building an optimal portfolio and as such I consider it to be one of the ten cornerstone principles of asset allocation.

Diversification

A strategy designed to reduce total risk by combining a large number of securities within a particular asset class that exhibit similar risk and return trade-off profiles.

The strategy of diversification is not underscored by the trade-off between risk and return. Rather it is underscored by the concept that as you add more securities with essentially the same risk and return trade-off profile, the less each security, in regards to company-specific risk, will impact the overall portfolio. The goal of diversification is to minimize company-specific risk, thus leaving a portfolio with only market risk.

Example: If the Smith Foundation held 5 securities in its portfolio and one of those securities were negatively impacted by a company-specific event, then 20% of the portfolio would be impacted. However, if the Smith Foundation held 25 securities and one of the securities were negatively impacted by a company-specific event, then only 4% of the portfolio would be impacted.

The following charts illustrate the benefits of diversification. As you add more securities to your portfolio, your total risk declines. Twenty or more securities in a portfolio is said to achieve diversification.

FIGURE 2.10

Benefit of Diversification

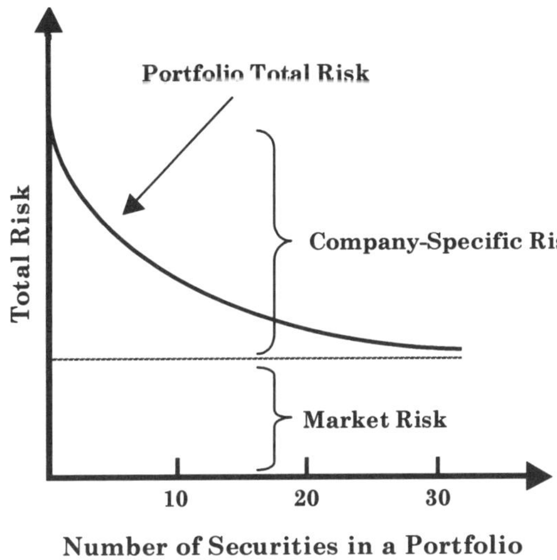

FIGURE 2.11

Diversification Impact on a Hypothetical Efficient Frontier

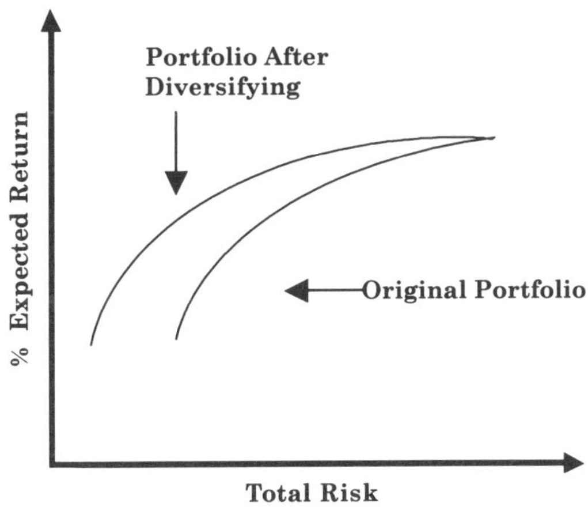

As you can see from the figures on the preceding page, as you add more securities to your portfolio, your total portfolio risk declines.

Only those securities with essentially the same risk and return trade-off profile should be purchased otherwise the risk and return trade-off profile of your overall portfolio will change. Obviously, finding individual securities with the same risk and return trade-off profile is not easy. An alternative to finding individual securities is to purchase an index investment. Thus, in one fell swoop you can achieve proper diversification without the hassle and added transaction and research costs from purchasing numerous securities.

Impact of Time Horizon

Your time horizon is another very important input variable. Most investors pay too little attention to time horizon and the important role it plays. Your time horizon impacts:

- Expected rates of return
- Expected volatility
- Expected asset class correlations

As a result of the important role it plays, time horizon is the first constraint that should be determined. Overestimating or underestimating your time horizon can significantly impact your risk and return trade-off profile.

The primary role time horizon plays is to help you select and evaluate the appropriateness of each asset class and asset subclass as an investment alternative. Specifically, time horizon helps to determine your balance between equity investments and investments that emphasize current income, namely fixed-income securities and cash & equivalents. The shorter your time horizon the more emphasis you should place on current income investments. Conversely, the longer your time horizon the more emphasis you should place on equities. Why? In the short-term, equities are simply too volatile and posses high levels of uncertainty. Said another way, equities exhibit unacceptable levels of risk in relation to their expected returns. On the other hand, fixed-income securities and cash & equivalents are significantly less volatile in the short-term and posses much lower levels of uncertainty. As a consequence, their risks in relation to their expected returns are more favorable in the short-term.

As your investment time horizon increases, so to does the probability of your equity assets experiencing positive returns. Why? The reason is because over longer periods of time equity returns become more stable since there is more time for positive equity returns to offset negative equity returns. The returns of equities become significantly more clear and predictable as your investment time horizon lengthens. Figure 2.12 illustrates this point.

FIGURE 2.12

Probability of Equities Outperforming Fixed Income Securities Given the Following Holding Periods.

Holding Period in Years	Probability of Equities Outperforming Fixed-Income
1	62%
3	75%
5	78%
10	91%
25	100%

Source: Calculated by the Frush Financial Group based on data supplied by the Center for Research in Security Prices at the University of Chicago over the period 1950-2002. Equities selected are small cap stocks. Fixed-income selected are 30-year U.S. government bonds.

FIGURE 2.13

Relationship Between Time Horizon and Portfolio Balance

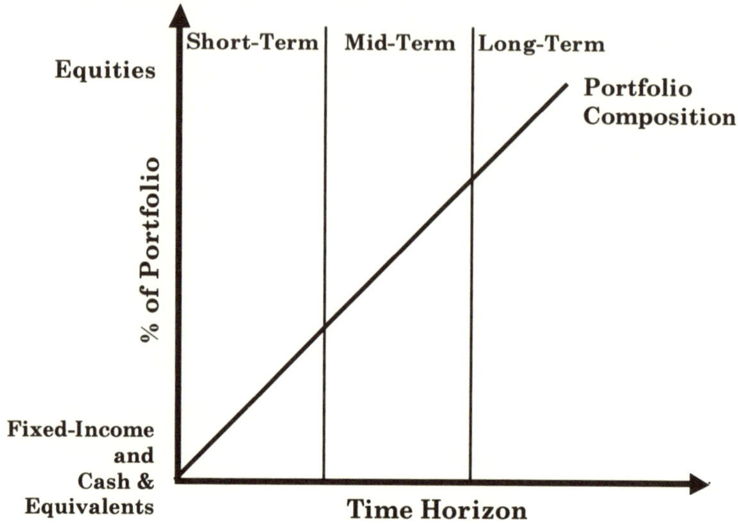

Counter-Argument of Asset Allocation

Since the goal of asset allocation is to maximize your expected total rate of return for the level of risk you are willing and able to assume, it is possible for you to earn higher returns without using asset allocation by assuming substantially greater risk. For example, you may decide to invest in an asset class based purely on its expected return. Doing so does not take into account the risk of the asset class. Thus, if the market advances the actual return of the portfolio will be higher than the overall market. On the flip side, if the market declines, then the actual returns of the portfolio will lag the market. Why? The reason is because you have decided to hold more risky assets. More risky assets provide higher return potential, but also higher risk potential.

Depending on the situation, the results from applying asset allocation will vary. Under certain circumstances, a portfolio's investment return may be higher or lower than expected simply given changes to some important factors. These factors include the following:

- Movement in correlations among asset classes
- Abnormal asset class strength or weakness
- Changing investor objectives and constraints
- Establishing an appropriate optimal asset mix
- Flexibility of allocations within the optimal asset mix
- Asset allocation strategy selected
- Skill in rebalancing

Chapter 3

Asset Classes Explained

♦ ♦ ♦

Introduction to Asset Classes

An asset class is a group of securities that share similar underlying characteristics as well as very similar risk and return trade-off profiles. As a result of their similarities, the market prices of securities within each asset class tend to move together. The market price for each security within an asset class is highly influenced by events involving other securities within the asset class or the asset class as a whole. Whether justified or not, even one security can greatly influence the prices for the other securities within the asset class. Asset classes are sometimes referred to as investment classes.

The four primary asset classes include:

- Equity assets
- Fixed-income assets
- Cash & equivalents assets
- Alternative assets

Each asset class can be divided into asset subclasses, such as large and small market capitalization equity securities or taxable and tax-exempt fixed-income securities.

Market Capitalization

The total market value of a publicly traded company. Calculated by multiplying the number of shares outstanding by the market price per share.

As with the primary asset classes, each asset subclass is distinguished by its own unique risk and return characteristics. The benefit of asset subclasses is it's less than perfect correlations to other asset classes, but more specifically to other asset subclasses. Thus, you can add different asset subclasses to your portfolio to enhance your portfolio's risk and return trade-off profile. For instance, a portfolio with both international and U.S. large capitalization equity securities will exhibit a more ideal risk and return trade-off profile than a portfolio comprising only international large capitalization equity securities. Asset subclasses can be thought of as providing enhanced asset allocation or asset allocation within the primary asset classes.

Characteristics of Asset Classes

As mentioned previously, securities within each asset class share similar underlying characteristics. Each characteristic allows for portfolio customization. This is beneficial since different investors have different needs. But what are the underlying characteristics within each asset class?

The most important underlying characteristics include the following:

- Total return potential
- Price volatility
- Correlation to other asset classes and asset subclasses
- Growth vs. income trade-off
- Liquidity
- Market efficiency
- Factors that influence their market value
- Type of underlying entity (corporation, government)

FIGURE 3.1

Historical Returns from December 31, 1941 – December 31, 2002

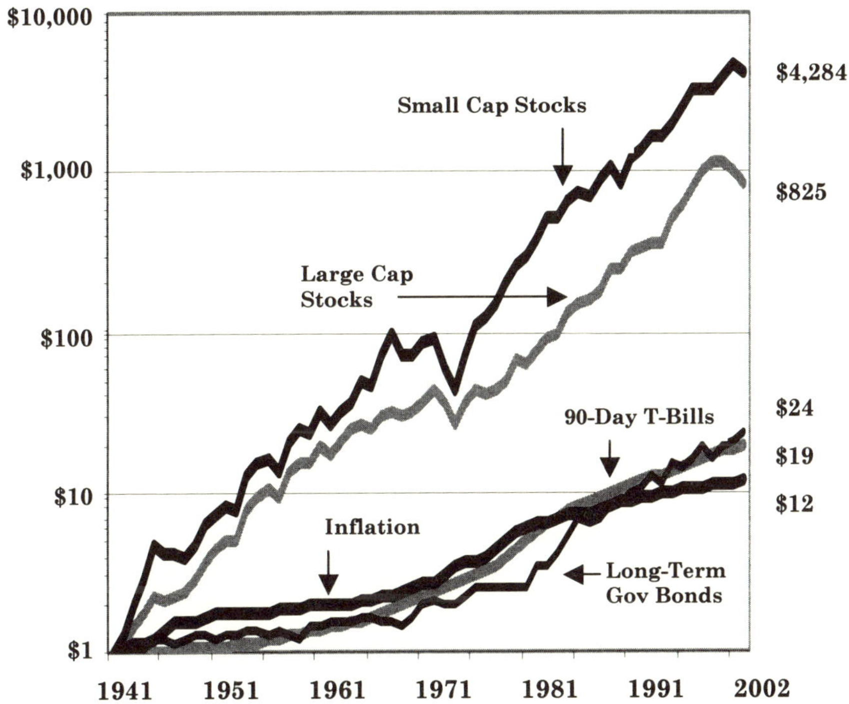

Source: Center for Research in Security Prices at the University of Chicago.

Equity Assets

Equity assets represent an ownership interest in a corporation and signify a claim to a corporation's assets. In order to fund business operations, corporations first raise capital by issuing equity securities. Each share of stock owned gives an investor a proportional share of the corporation's profits, which are usually distributed in the form of dividends. In addition, owners of most equity securities are given voting rights. Voting rights allow you, for instance, to vote for a corporation's Board of Directors, approve or disapprove of employee stock option programs and vote for or against acquisitions. From my experience, individual investors foolishly do not exercise their right to vote. In response, more power shifts to corporate management shareholders and to large institutions. Each has their own agenda, which typically isn't always on the same page as individual investors. Remember to always exercise your right to vote.

There are essentially two types of equity securities: preferred stock and common stock.

Preferred stock

Contrary to some beliefs, preferred stock is considered an equity security rather than a fixed-income security. The misconception is understandable since many investors buy preferred stock for the dividends rather than the price appreciation.

Preferred stock represents ownership of a corporation, but is slightly different from common stock. Preferred stock shareholders do not have voting rights. In exchange, shareholders receive a higher priority on the assets of the corporation in the event of liquidation due to bankruptcy. Furthermore, it is commonplace for shareholders of preferred stock to receive not only a higher yielding dividend, but also priority in receiving dividends over that of common stock shareholders. For example, if a corporation is having difficulty in meeting their dividend payments to both preferred and common stock shareholders, the corporation must make dividend payments to the preferred stock shareholders first. Afterwards, providing enough cash remains, common stock shareholders will receive their dividend payments.

Cumulative Preferred

A preferred stock that has priority in receiving dividends over that of common stock. The cumulative provision obligates the corporation to pay all accumulated dividends before dividends can be made to the shareholders of common stock.

Lastly, many corporations issue what is called convertible preferred stock. This type of preferred is very similar to non-convertible preferred stock with one significant difference. Convertible preferred stock gives the owner the option to convert, or exchange, his or her preferred shares into a fixed number of common stock shares after a predetermined date. The market value of this type of preferred is more volatile since its value is influenced by the market value of the related common stock.

Common stock

Common stock is the most widely used form of equity ownership. Common stock shareholders have voting rights and often participate in receiving profits in the form of dividends. However, not all corporations distribute profits in the form of dividends. Rather, some reinvest the dividends back into their company in order to fund existing and planned operations.

Two of the most common asset subclasses are growth and value stocks. Again, each possesses its own unique risk and return trade-off profile. Both of these asset subclasses have similar characteristics with each other since they both are equity securities, however, they also have very important differences. As a result, growth and value stocks tend to have a low correlation to each other. It is a common misconception that growth companies and growth stocks are one in the same. But there is a difference.

Growth Stock

Common stock that produces higher rates of return than the stocks of its industry peers.

Value Stock

Common stock that is considered undervalued given its expected rate of return and present stock price.

Growth Company

A company that generates rates of return far in excess of their weighted average cost of capital. This allows most growth companies to generate higher rates of return on their invested capital than their peers.

FIGURE 3.2

Value Stocks and Growth Stocks

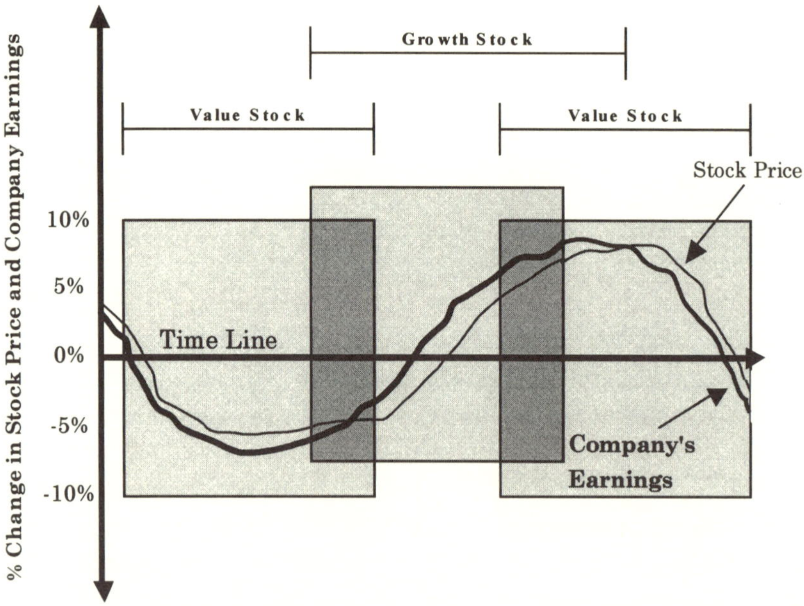

Intuitively, one can see how a particular security can be considered a value stock at one point in time and then be considered a growth stock at a later point of time.

FIGURE 3.3

Snapshot of Equity Assets

Most Common Asset Subclasses	Factors That Influence Returns
• Large market capitalization • Middle market capitalization • Small market capitalization • Growth stocks • Value stocks • Master limited partnerships • Securities of developed international markets • Securities of emerging international markets	• Overall market conditions • Company-specific characteristics, principally the present value of expected future cash flows • Valuations, as measured by price to sales, price to earnings, price to free cash flow, and price to tangible book value • Investors' behaviors, preferences and risk tolerances • Flow of funds
Positives	**Negatives**
• High total return potential • Ownership (participation in capital appreciation and voting) • Numerous asset subclasses to enhance the risk and return trade-off profile and to satisfy different investor preferences • Liquid and efficient market	• High risk potential • Low current income potential (dividends) • Difficult to forecast risk and return • Fluctuating correlations

FIGURE 3.4

Historical Returns for Equity Securities from December 31, 1925 – December 31, 2002

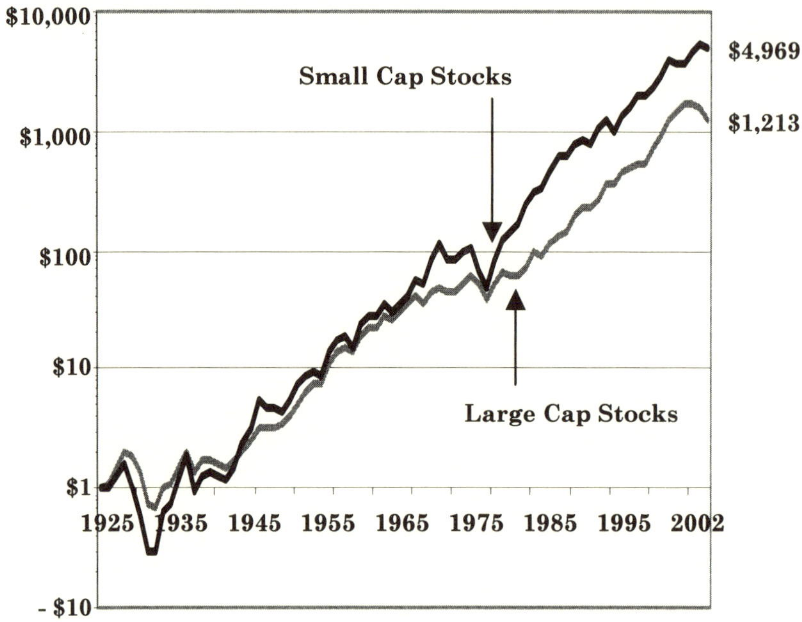

Source: Center for Research in Security Prices at the University of Chicago.

Fixed-Income Assets

Fixed-income assets represent a loan to a corporation or governmental entity in order to raise capital. Fixed-income assets are commonly referred to as debt in the investment community. In most cases, assets of the issuer back each fixed-income security, thus providing the purchaser with some protection in the case of default. These assets, or debt instruments, hold the issuer to a contractual obligation to make periodic interest payments to the purchaser on predetermined dates in predetermined amounts until the security reaches maturity or is called by the issuer.

Maturity

The date on which an issuer is obligated to pay the principal of a fixed-income security to the purchaser.

Called

An event where a fixed-income security is redeemed by the issuer prior to maturity.

Typically, the longer the time to maturity for a fixed-income security the higher its yield tends to be. Thus, short-term securities typically have lower yields than do long-term securities.

Yield

The annual rate of return determined by dividing the annual interest payments by the purchase price or market value (depending on when and how you are evaluating the security).

For a real world example, simply look at cash & equivalents. Cash & equivalents do have many similarities with fixed-income securities, however, the one characteristic that defines them as cash & equivalents rather than fixed-income is their short-term maturity. But why do securities with longer maturities have higher yields? The principal and most accepted theory (since there are other theories) says that investors demand higher rates of return for each progressively longer period of time because they must forego current consumption of the money they invest and assume risk for a longer period of time than if the holding period were shorter.

To illustrate how investors demand higher rates of return for securities with longer maturities, the yield curve was created.

Yield Curve

A representation of the relationship between fixed-income yields and their time to maturity.

FIGURE 3.5

Standard Yield Curve

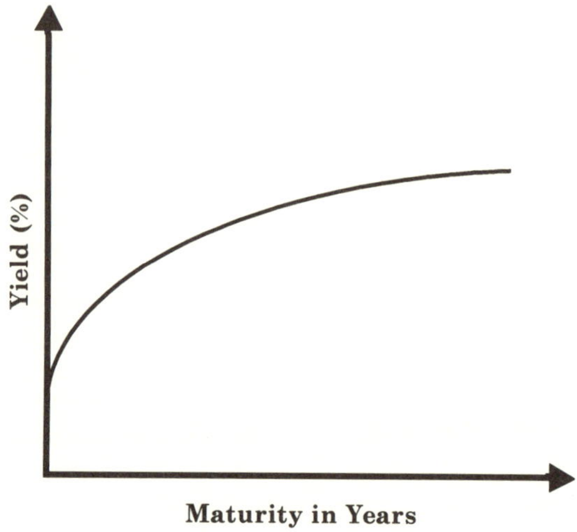

FIGURE 3.6

Snapshot of Fixed-Income Assets

Most Common Asset Subclasses	Factors That Influence Returns
• U.S. treasury notes and bonds • State securities • Municipal securities • Government agency securities • Corporate bonds • Mortgaged backed securities • Asset backed securities	• Macroeconomic forecasts • Fiscal and monetary policies • Rate of inflation (or deflation) • Flow of funds • Investors' behaviors, preferences and risk tolerances • Supply and demand

Positives	Negatives
• Low risk potential	• Low return potential
• Tax advantages	• Interest rate risk
• Low correlations to other asset classes	• Default risk
• Government securities are considered default free	• Prepayment risk
• Priority of claims on assets	• Higher transaction costs
	• Liquidity risk
	• Greater price inefficiencies

FIGURE 3.7

Historical Returns for Fixed-Income Assets from December 31, 1941 – December 31, 2002

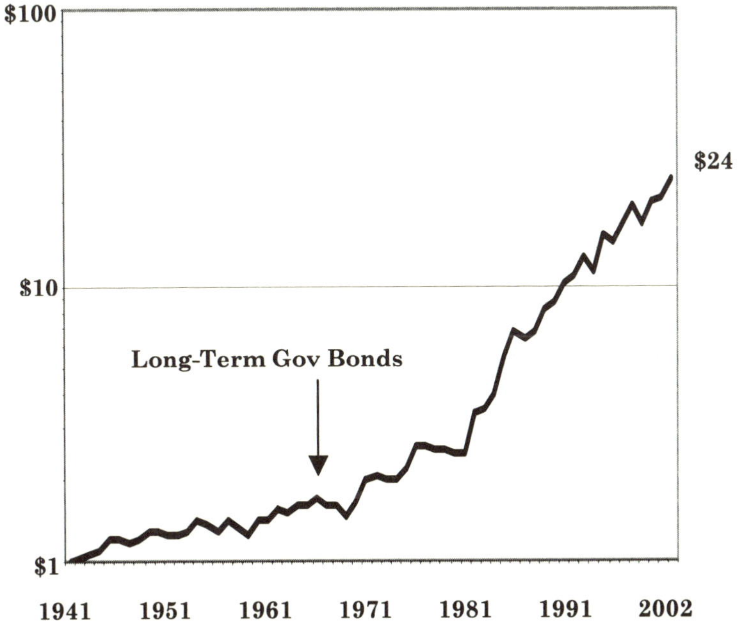

Source: Center for Research in Security Prices at the University of Chicago.

Cash & Equivalents Assets

Cash & equivalents assets are a very broad category defining those assets that are highly liquid, very safe and can be converted easily into cash, such as money market funds, or are already in that form, such as coins and bills. Cash & equivalents usually have a maturity date within one year. The returns of this asset class generally correlate to the rate of inflation. Thus, as inflation rates fall so to do the rates on money market funds and certificates of deposit. Cash & equivalents are differentiated by their issuer, maturity date, interest rate (referred to as coupon rate), credit quality, and tax status (taxable or non-taxable).

FIGURE 3.8

Snapshot of Cash & Equivalents Assets

Most Common Asset Subclasses	Factors That Influence Returns
• Coins, bills and related • Bank holdings • U.S. treasury bills • Money market funds • Certificates of deposit	• Rate of inflation (or deflation) • Flow of funds • Supply and demand • Macroeconomic forecasts • Fiscal and monetary policies
Positives	**Negatives**
• Very low risk potential • The most current and predictable income • Safety of principal • Quick access to funds	• Low returns • Purchasing power risk • Reinvestment risk • Small but existent default risk

FIGURE 3.9

Historical Returns for Cash & Equivalents Assets from December 31, 1925 – December 31, 2002

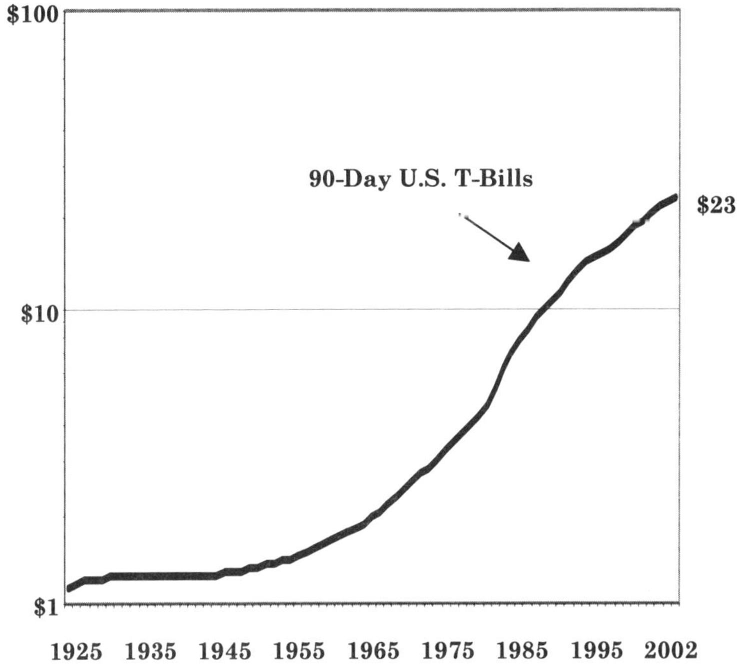

Source: Center for Research in Security Prices at the University of Chicago.

Alternative Assets

Alternative assets comprise a very broad category of assets, mostly encompassing what are referred to as hard assets. In contrast to the other primary asset classes, alternative assets are more dissimilar in their inherent characteristics than they are similar. Furthermore, most alternative assets are tangible, rather than intangible, as they are with the other primary asset classes.

The principle reason underlying the purchase of alternative assets is to hedge inflation. In practice this is referred to as protecting your purchasing power. Another strong reason to invest in alternative assets is because they tend to have very low, and sometimes negative, correlations with equities. Alternative assets do well in times of high inflation and often capture more investment inflows during time of market weakness, regardless of their valuation.

FIGURE 3.10

Snapshot of Alternative Assets

Most Common Asset Subclasses	Factors That Influence Returns
• Real estate • Commodities (including precious metals) • Private equity • Hedge funds • Art	• Supply and demand • Flow of funds • Rate of inflation (or deflation) • Regulatory issues • Currency exchange rates • Transaction costs • Shipping and holding costs

Given the vast dissimilarities among the different assets that comprise alternative assets, a breakout of each alternative asset's positives and negatives is necessary.

Real estate

Real estate can be defined as land, including the air above and the ground below, the permanent buildings or structures attached and all the natural resources contained within the domain. Essentially you have two avenues to invest in real estate. First, you can buy real estate directly using funds from your investment portfolio (at this time funds from a retirement portfolio cannot be used for this purpose although there has been significant headway to permit it). Second, you can invest in REITs, or real estate investment trusts. REITs are very similar to mutual funds, or more specifically closed-end mutual funds, in that you buy shares of a portfolio of real estate.

FIGURE 3.11

Positives and Negatives of Real Estate

Positives	Negatives
• Significant tax advantages • Low correlations to the other asset classes • High current income potential	• High transaction costs • Greater market inefficiencies • Liquidity concerns

Commodities

Commodities can be defined as tangible articles of trade, such as agricultural products or metals, which are indistinguishable and thus interchangeable with each other. Finally, commodities are processed and resold.

FIGURE 3.12

Positives and Negatives of Commodities

Positives	Negatives
• Hedge against inflation • Low correlations to other asset classes • Ability to leverage highly	• Greatly impacted by geopolitical events • Highly volatile

Private equity

Private equity can be defined as capital exchanged for shares of a private business.

FIGURE 3.13

Positives and Negatives of Private Equity

Positives	Negatives
• Significant return potential • Low correlations to the other asset classes • Ability to focus investments to desired industry segments	• Substantial risk • Regulatory concerns • Marginal liquidity

Hedge funds

Hedge funds can be defined as private funds where investments are made using aggressive strategies. Such strategies include short selling, significant leverage, computer program trading, derivatives and swaps. By law, hedge funds are restricted to a low number of investors. As a result, the vast majority of hedge funds only target institutions and wealthy individuals.

FIGURE 3.14

Positives and Negatives of Hedge Funds

Positives	Negatives
• High return potential • Low correlations to the other asset classes • Multiple styles	• High management fees • Substantial risk • Tax concerns

Art

For purposes of this book, art is defined as a painting, sculpture, or other creative object that can be purchased and sold by a willing buyer and seller for reasons in addition to their aesthetic beauty. As you know, you cannot hold art in your portfolio like you can real estate (via REITs) and commodities (via indices). However, art can be purchased with funds that would otherwise be earmarked for your portfolio.

FIGURE 3.15

Positives and Negatives of Art

Positives	Negatives
• Low correlations to the other asset classes • Aesthetic gratification • Low risk	• Inefficient market • Illiquid market • Investor preferences

Understanding each asset class, its expected risk and return trade-off profile and the correlations among the classes is essential to asset allocation theory and its application to your investment portfolio. Asset classes represent building blocks for the selection of appropriate investments and their weightings within your portfolio.

Given the different asset classes available, you can customize your portfolio in a way most appropriate to achieve your objectives and constraints. Utilizing each asset class is central to enhancing your portfolio's return while reducing its risk. Consider a football team for example. A team comprised only of linemen will most likely not reach the playoffs. Odds are they won't even win a game! It takes a well-balanced team with players from all positions to reach the championship game. Building an optimal portfolio requires this same approach.

Benefits of a Multi-Class Portfolio

The following chart illustrates the benefits of allocating a portfolio's assets to two asset classes rather than allocating only to one asset class.

FIGURE 3.16

Benefits of a Multi-Class Portfolio

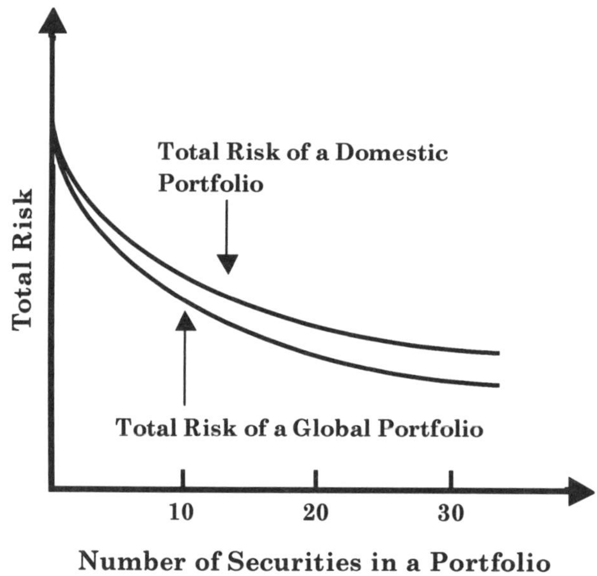

Historical Correlations

The chart on the following page illustrates the historical correlations between asset classes observed between 1926 and 2002. The lower the correlation between two assets the greater the return enhancing and risk reducing benefits are from investing in both assets.

FIGURE 3.17

Correlation of Annual Returns from December 31, 1925 – December 31, 2002

	Large Cap Stocks	Small Cap Stocks	U.S. Treasury Bills	Long-Term U.S. Gov Bonds	Inflation (CPI)
Large Cap Stocks	1.00	0.87	0.02	0.13	*
Small Cap Stocks		1.00	-0.01	0.09	*
U.S. Treasury Bills			1.00	0.23	0.24
Long-Term U.S. Gov Bonds				1.00	-0.02
Inflation (CPI)					1.00

* Slightly negative – close to zero

Source: Calculated by the Frush Financial Group based on data supplied by the Center for Research in Security Prices at the University of Chicago

Selecting Asset Classes for Investment

One of the most critical decisions involving assets classes is how best to balance the equity asset class with both the fixed-income and cash & equivalents asset classes, or what are referred to as current income producing asset classes for their ability to generate income in the form of dividends and interest. Why? The simple reason is the low correlations all other asset classes have with the equity asset class. The chart on the next page provides a framework for how best to select asset classes given your objectives and constraints. When reading the chart, first locate your objective or constraint for the corresponding category (time horizon, risk tolerance, etc) and then determine if your portfolio should emphasize current income producing asset classes or the equity asset class.

FIGURE 3.18

Selecting Asset Classes for Investment

Your Objective or Constraint	Emphasize Current Income Producing Asset Classes *When*	Emphasize Equity Assets *When*
Time Horizon	Short-term time horizon	Long-term time horizon
Risk Tolerance	Low risk tolerance	High risk tolerance
Current Income Needs	High income needs	Low current income needs
Purchasing Power Protection	Low purchasing power needs	High purchasing power needs
Economic Trend	Declining	Rising

Thus, an investor with a low risk tolerance should emphasize current income producing assets while an investor with a long-term time horizon should emphasize equity assets.

In addition to using the above chart, please see Appendix A for a worksheet on how best to identify your optimal asset mix.

FIGURE 3.19

Summary of Asset Class Return and Risk Potentials.

Asset Class	Return Potential	Risk Potential
Equities	Moderate to High	Moderate to High
Fixed-income	Low to Moderate	Low to Moderate
Cash & Equivalents	Low	Low
Alternatives	Low, Moderate or High	Low, Moderate or High

Chapter 4

Asset Allocation Strategies

♦ ♦ ♦

Introduction to Asset Allocation Strategies

Determining your asset allocation strategy is almost as important as determining your optimal asset mix. Asset allocation strategies are the foundation of rebalancing, one of the cornerstone principles of asset allocation.

Asset Allocation Strategy
Defines how and when a portfolio should be rebalanced given deviations of a portfolio's asset mix from its optimal asset mix. Also referred to as rebalancing strategy.

Rebalancing

The process of selling and buying investments in order to return the current asset class weightings to the weightings as defined by the optimal asset mix.

Types of Asset Allocation Strategies

There are a number of different asset allocation strategies available to you. Some are more common while others are the inventions and proprietary use of financial services firms. The two most common strategies in use by the financial community include:

- Strategic
- Tactical

Two other well-known, but less employed, strategies are integrated asset allocation and insured asset allocation. Although this book will not cover them to the extent of strategic and tactical asset allocation due to their more infrequent use, I'd like to quickly define them for you. Integrated asset allocation is a strategy whereby you periodically change your optimal asset mix depending on changes to either your objectives and constraints or market conditions. This strategy is essentially a combination of strategic asset allocation and tactical asset allocation. Insured asset allocation is a strategy whereby you change your optimal asset mix is response to your changing risk tolerance, which is thought to rise as you age and accumulate more wealth. As a result, your allocation to equities rises at the expense of cash and equivalents. In addition, your optimal asset mix could change to include a greater allocation to cash and equivalents if the total market value of your portfolio declines due to market weakness. Why? The reason is because your wealth declined and this strategy is based exclusively on your level of wealth. Let's shift our focus to the two asset allocation strategies most employed by financial services firms.

Strategic asset allocation

Strategic asset allocation can be thought of as a passive long-term strategy. This strategy is appropriate for all investors and under all market conditions, both bull and bear.

Strategic Asset Allocation

A strategy whereby the asset classes within a portfolio are rebalanced when their weightings either move above their allocation range ceilings or below their allocation range floors.

Do not confuse strategic asset allocation with the philosophy of "buy and hold". Under the buy and hold philosophy, a portfolio is created and no revisions are made to your portfolio's asset mix during the holding period. Over time, price movements will alter (sometimes substantially) the asset mix of your portfolio. As a result, you will have a portfolio that either exhibits greater risk than appropriate since the portfolio is over allocated to one asset class or experiences a lower actual total return than expected since the portfolio does not receive the return enhancing benefits derived from multi-class investing. In either case, the portfolio is not optimal. Lastly, any market weakness will have a magnified effect since some asset classes will be disproportionately too large given no rebalancing. As you can see, a buy and hold strategy conflicts with the underlying philosophy of rebalancing.

When designing your portfolio, the appropriate asset classes are first selected followed by their optimal weightings. Over time, the price of each asset class fluctuates, either up or down depending on market forces. As a result, the asset class weightings will change. For instance, if fixed-income prices experience significant strength, then fixed-income assets, as a percentage of the overall portfolio, will rise while the other asset class weightings, as percentages of the overall portfolio, will fall, all else being equal.

During the rebalancing phase, you will do one or both of the following:

- Sell asset classes where their current weighting is above their allocation range ceiling and reallocate the proceeds to the other asset classes.
- Buy asset classes where their current weighting is below their allocation range floor. To obtain the funds necessary to accomplish this task you will need to sell a portion of the remaining asset classes.

Example: The Smith portfolio was designed with an optimal asset mix of 60% equities, 30% fixed-income, and 10% cash & equivalents. Due to a surge in equity prices, one year later the portfolio was comprised of 75% equities, 20% fixed-income and 5% cash & equivalents. Under strategic asset allocation, the portfolio manager will sell equities, or approximately 15% (75%-60%) of the portfolio's market value, and reinvest the proceeds in fixed-income and cash & equivalents. Doing so will return the portfolio to the optimal asset mix of 60%, 30%, and 10% for equities, fixed-income and cash & equivalents, respectively.

Portfolio managers often establish asset class allocation ranges via floors and ceilings. As long as asset class weightings move within their respective allocation ranges portfolio managers generally will take no action. However, if an asset class weighting moves above the ceiling or below the floor the portfolio manager will generally rebalance the portfolio. I say 'generally rebalance' since all rebalancing decisions must be made within the context of their costs. This consideration will be covered in the monitoring and rebalancing chapter.

Example: The Jones portfolio has an optimal asset mix of 50% equities, 40% fixed-income and 10% cash & equivalents. The portfolio manager establishes an equity ceiling at 60% and a floor at 40%. One year later the equity weighting reaches 61%.

In response, the portfolio manager sells equities equal to 11% (61%-50%) of the portfolio and buys fixed-income and cash & equivalents thus returning the portfolio to the optimal asset mix of 50% equities, 40% fixed-income and 10% cash and equivalents.

Strategic asset allocation places little to no importance on market changes while investors' objectives and constraints are thought to remain constant during the holding period. Under certain circumstances, however, your optimal asset mix may need to be changed. These circumstances include:

- Material changes to your objectives and constraints
- Material changes to the risk and return trade-off profile of an asset class within your portfolio

Depending on the degree of change to one or both of the above circumstances, you will need to alter your optimal asset mix proportionately. For instance, if your risk tolerance declines slightly, then you will need to change your optimal asset mix slightly by allocating a greater amount to less risky assets. This may involve reducing your equity allocation and increasing either your allocation to fixed-income or cash & equivalents.

Tactical asset allocation

Tactical asset allocation is a form of market timing, the goal of which is to produce higher returns by capitalizing on short-term price movements. Tactical asset allocation is founded on the notion that the market is inefficient to some degree and that skillful portfolio managers can profit from these inefficiencies. In other words, this strategy attempts to "beat the market".

Tactical Asset Allocation

A market timing strategy whereby the portfolio's optimal asset mix and allocation ranges are intentionally changed with the goal of capturing short-term profits.

Under this strategy, you will deliberately either increase or decrease your optimal asset mix and allocation ranges in response to current and anticipated future asset class price movements. Contrary to strategic asset allocation, under tactical asset allocation, an asset class showing strength may be allowed to 'run', so to speak, by adjusting the optimal asset mix and allocation range ceiling upward. In so doing, you hope to profit from the upward movement of the particular asset class, which would have been rebalanced under strategic asset allocation.

Example: The Smith portfolio was designed with an optimal asset mix of 60% equities and 40% fixed-income. Furthermore, the portfolio was designed with allocation ranges of 55%-65% for equities and 35%-45% for fixed-income. Subsequent to portfolio design, equities experience price weakness while fixed-income experience price strength. As a result, the asset allocation of the portfolio changes to 50% equities and 50% fixed-income. Under strategic asset allocation the portfolio manager will need to rebalance the Smith portfolio as both equities and fixed-income have deviated outside of their allocation ranges. However, under tactical asset allocation, the portfolio manager could adjust the portfolio's allocation ranges to forgo rebalancing. The goal of such an adjustment is to capture short-term profits from rising fixed-income prices. To accomplish this change, the portfolio manager might adjust the allocation ranges to 45%-55% for equities and 45%-55% for fixed-income.

With tactical asset allocation, portfolio managers employ a number of different methods to find market inefficiencies and to determine when and how to profit from them. One of the most common methods is to analyze the business cycle and create a forecast based on multiple possible future economic scenarios. The result of this forecast is then used to produce expected returns for each asset class. Comparisons of their expected returns for each asset class are measured against market expectations with actions to exploit any variations then made.

Although this strategy is an asset allocation strategy, remember that the focus of tactical asset allocation is to profit from market timing. As we know, market timing determines only a small fraction of total investment performance over time.

Which Strategy Should You Employ?

Selecting an asset allocation strategy is dependent on the following two expectations:

- Whether your objectives and constraints are expected to remain constant or change during the holding period.
- Whether the risk and return trade-off profiles for each asset class are expected to remain constant or to change during the holding period.

The following chart will help you determine which strategy is appropriate given the above expectations.

FIGURE 4.1

Selecting an Asset Allocation Strategy

Your Objectives and Constraints	Risk & Return Trade-off Profiles	Strategy
Constant	Constant	Strategic
Constant	*Changing*	Strategic or Tactical
Changing	Constant	Strategic or Tactical
Changing	*Changing*	Strategic

As for my recommendation, I am a proponent of strategic asset allocation and suggest you emphasize it. By selecting tactical asset allocation you are simply betting that you can beat the market.

Part 2

Applying Asset Allocation

Chapter 5

Establishing Your Objectives and Constraints

♦ ♦ ♦

Importance of Establishing Your Objectives and Constraints

Now that we have discussed the importance and theories behind asset allocation, we shift gears and address how you should apply asset allocation theory to build your optimal portfolio.

The process of applying asset allocation begins with identifying your specific financial goals. These goals may include the creation of a cash emergency fund, retiring at age 60, purchasing a summer home or taking a trip around the world upon retirement. Once your specific financial goals have been identified, attention is given to establishing what we call in the investment field, objectives and constraints. Establishing your objectives and constraints is the formal process of setting the foundation upon which your optimal portfolio can then be designed. In practice, objectives are usually expressed in terms of return aspiration and risk tolerance while constraints are usually expressed as time horizon, liquidity needs, tax considerations, legal and regulatory considerations and unique circumstances and preferences.

Your objectives and constraints are the driving force underlying the process of managing your portfolio. To build your optimal portfolio, you will need to establish clear, measurable and achievable objectives and constraints. In doing so, you will be able to determine which asset classes and asset subclasses to include in your portfolio and in what proportion.

Objectives and Constraints Explained

Return aspiration

Return aspiration can be viewed as the desired financial reward sought by you for deferring current consumption and making an investment. The reward for making an investment can come in two forms: appreciation of principle and receiving dividends and interest income.

It would seem intuitive to assume that your return aspiration is infinite. However, in practice, you need to establish return aspirations that are in balance with the level of risk you are willing and able to assume.

Return aspirations are established in response to your specific financial goals, such as needing $15,000 for college tuition in five years or needing $40,000 in dividends and interest per year to support your lifestyle in retirement.

When establishing your return aspiration, your specific financial goals need to be prioritized and quantified. Simply saying you need enough money to fund a college education is simply too vague and not prudent. Furthermore, your return aspiration needs to be realistic; it should neither be vague nor unattainable.

Once a list of specific financial goals has been made, your risk tolerance should then be determined. Since the overall goal of asset allocation is to maximize expected total return for a given level of risk assumed, you should compare and contrast your specific goals with your risk tolerance. Based on this evaluation, you will gain a more accurate recognition of your return aspiration.

Risk tolerance

Risk tolerance is one of the most important inputs to the portfolio management process. Although there are different definitions of risk, it is generally defined as uncertainty in regards to a future outcome. Uncertainty can come in the form of price volatility or actual investment results not matching expected investment results. Your risk tolerance is primarily based on your:

- Wealth level
- Income and expenses
- Unique personal preferences

Some investors can tolerate an above average amount of volatility if they have a better chance of actual results matching expected results while others cannot stomach large swings in total portfolio market value from quarter to quarter. Since you cannot control whether or not actual results match expected results, risk tolerance is based primarily on your tolerance for volatility. As mentioned in chapter two, volatility, as a measure of risk, is important because the more volatile a security both the greater the chances are to experience a severe negative result and the lower probability that you may not achieve a specific expected rate of return.

Determining your volatility tolerance is rather subjective and therefore difficult to express as a measurable input. Miscalculating your volatility tolerance can have significant negative consequences on your portfolio. A good way to determine your risk tolerance is to complete a risk tolerance questionnaire. Most financial services firms offer them to their clients. Appendix A of this book provides a risk tolerance worksheet for your use.

Time horizon

As mentioned in chapter two, time horizon is a key input to the asset allocation process. As such, I consider time horizon as one of the cornerstone principles of asset allocation. Time horizon greatly impacts expectations for asset class returns, asset class volatility and correlations among asset classes.

FIGURE 5.1

Relationship Between Time Horizon and Portfolio Composition

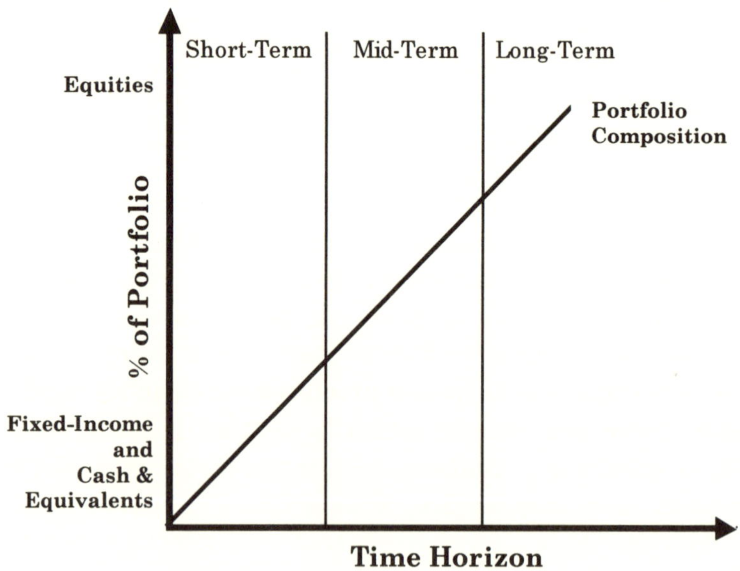

The primary use of time horizon is to help determine the portfolio balance between equities and asset classes that emphasize current income over capital appreciation. The asset classes that fall within this category are fixed-income and cash & equivalents. All else being equal, the longer your time horizon the more equity assets and less current income producing assets you should incorporate.

The most prevalent risk for any investment depends on your time horizon. The most prevalent type of risk you need to address over the long-term is purchasing power risk, or the loss in an asset's real value due to inflation. Equity investments provide the best defense against this type of risk. In the short-term, the most prevalent risk is price volatility. Fixed-income investments provide the best defense against this type of risk.

Many investors have a tendency to underestimate their time horizon. Time horizon is the period of time from the present to the future point in time when the assets in the portfolio are no longer needed. Two examples of why an investor will no longer need his or her assets include having more assets than needed to cover his or her everyday expenses or the death of the investor. Unfortunately, many investors view the ending point of their time horizon as their retirement age. Doing so does not take into account their retirement years, which can often be 30 plus years.

Liquidity needs

Liquidity needs can be defined as the degree to which you require cash to accomplish everyday activities and make special purchases. Consider, for example, a retired couple who use their investment portfolio to fund their retirement. In this situation, the retired couple would have a much higher liquidity need than would a couple in their prime income earning years where their income exceeds their expenses. As a result, the retired couple would need to build a portfolio that emphasizes income-oriented investments.

There are four primary categories of liquidity needs, presented below in order of importance:

- **Emergency cash:** Having an emergency cash fund is by far the most important liquidity need you have. Conventional wisdom says this fund should amount to anywhere between three to six months of your average monthly expenses.
- **Special needs:** Special needs are essentially those purchases or expenditures that are planned sometime within the next three to eight years. Examples include a second home or a grandchild's tuition.
- **Taxes:** There are two major taxes you will need to plan for, income taxes and estate taxes. Regardless of which tax, Uncle Sam wants his money quickly, within twelve months for income taxes and within nine months of death for estate taxes.
- **Savings and investments:** Savings and investments should not be mistaken for emergency cash. Each has its own purpose. Savings and investments allow you to take advantage of excess cash by forgoing current consumption and earning a return by putting it to work.

Tax considerations

This constraint deals with the complex role of realizing, deferring and avoiding taxes and how these tax issues impact your portfolio.

Tax management has become one of the hot new buzzwords in the portfolio management field. Why? Because the tax on capital gains can withhold almost a fifth of your investment return. In response, taxes are one of the many inputs that are employed when evaluating an investment for feasibility. As the number and complexity of your tax issues increase, so to does the need to involve either a CPA or an estate planning attorney.

There are a number of tax considerations you should address:

- **Capital gains:** Capital gains taxes are those taxes on the appreciation of an investment. Decisions to liquidate investments need to be evaluated with respect to their specific tax implications. However, investment decisions take utmost priority over tax considerations. For example, it is not prudent to hold an inappropriate investment just to defer the capital gains tax. You'd be surprised at the number of portfolio managers who do this unfortunately. Moreover, you'd be shocked at the number of portfolio managers who do not sell inappropriate investments simply because they do not want their clients to see their capital loss.
- **Growth vs. income:** As with capital gains, deciding between growth-oriented and income-oriented investments should first be made at the investment level and then evaluated with respect to their tax implications. Simply allocating more to growth-oriented investments in order to avoid taxes on current income is not prudent if you have a short-term time horizon.
- **Tax-exempt investments:** Depending on your tax rate, it may be ideal to substitute lower yielding tax-exempt government investments for higher yielding taxable investments. More specifically, municipal bonds for corporate bonds. Why? The reason is because the net after-tax return might be higher with lower yielding tax-exempt investments than with higher yielding taxable investments since the later is taxed. Adding more tax-exempt investments will decrease current income, but might increase your portfolio's total after-tax return.

In addition to the above tax considerations, you will need to be mindful of estate taxes, gift taxes, personal trust taxes and the Alternative Minimum Tax (AMT). These taxes are somewhat outside the topic of asset allocation and building a portfolio and are therefore not discussed in this book.

> *The hardest thing in the world to understand is the income tax.*
>
> – Albert Einstein

Legal and regulatory considerations

Legal and regulatory considerations are much more prevalent with institutional investors than with individual investors. However, some of the legal and regulatory considerations you may encounter involve:

- IRA contributions and withdrawals
- Employee stock option exercises
- Restricted stock
- Insider trading

In addition to the legal and regulatory considerations that involve individual investors, there are significantly more targeted to portfolio managers. Some of these considerations include:

- Insider trading
- Confidentiality of investor information
- Prudent management / appropriate investments

Unique circumstances and preferences

This constraint essentially incorporates anything that cannot be categorized in one of the other four constraints. Furthermore, many of the unique preferences are also considered here. Examples of unique circumstances and preferences include:

- Financially supporting a parent or adult child
- Preferring not to invest in military, tobacco or gun related companies

- Being physically or mentally disabled
- Filing for bankruptcy

Combination of Objectives and Constraints

The entire management of your optimal portfolio should occur where your objectives and constraints intersect. I term this intersection the OC Plane, which stands for objectives and constraints plane. This is an important concept and therefore represented in the definition of Optimal Investing. the strategy of employing time-honored and research backed principles and practices to protect and grow an investor's wealth *within the context of his or her objectives and constraints.* Time horizon, liquidity needs and regulatory issues can greatly impact the achievement of your objectives for instance. Each phase of the portfolio management process is dependent on balancing your objectives and constraints. As such, designing, constructing, monitoring and rebalancing all occur within the OC Plane. The figures on the following page will help you to visualize this concept.

FIGURE 5.2

Universe of Possible Objectives and Constraints

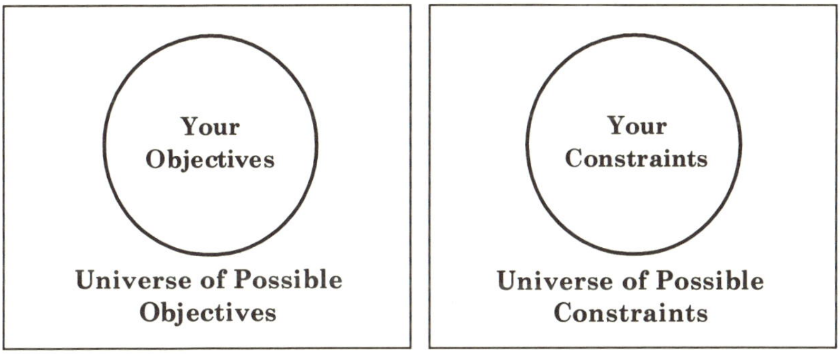

FIGURE 5.3

Intersection of Your Objectives and Constraints

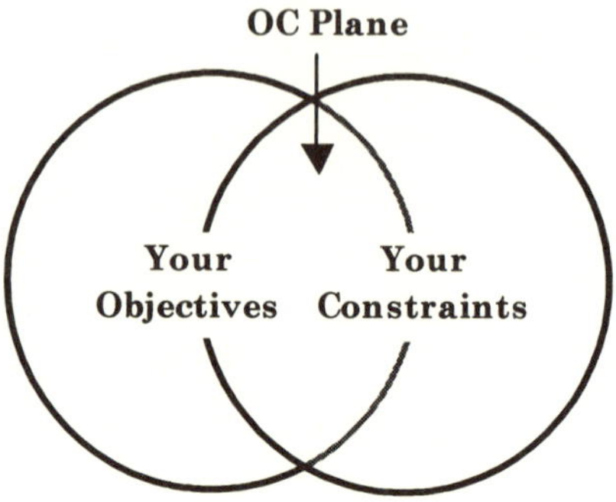

How to Establish Your Objectives & Constraints

The following seven steps provide a framework for establishing your objectives and constraints.

Step 1

Determine your investment time horizon. Again, this is the period from the present to the future point in time when you will no longer need the assets in your portfolio.

Step 2

Make a list of all of your specific financial goals during your investment time horizon. Remember, they need to be realistic, achievable and measurable.

Step 3

Determine your risk tolerance, or how much portfolio volatility you are willing and able to assume in order to achieve your specific financial goals. Appendix A will help you determine your risk tolerance.

Step 4

Determine how much liquidity you will need during your investment time horizon. Will 5% of your portfolio's assets in income-oriented assets be sufficient to cover your cash need or will 10% or even 15% be more appropriate?

Step 5

Determine what tax issues may arise during your investment time horizon and identify how you will effectively address them. Consider hiring a CPA if the issues are numerous and/or complex.

> *I have had a long, long life full of troubles, but there is one curious fact about them – nine-tenths of them never happened.*
>
> – Andrew Carnegie

Step 6

Determine what legal and regulatory issues may arise during your investment time horizon and identify how you will effectively address them. Estate planning attorneys and investment advisors can provide valuable insights if complex issues arise.

Step 7

Determine what, if any, unique circumstances and preferences you will need to address during your investment time horizon.

The 5 Biggest Mistakes Investors Make When Establishing Their Objectives & Constraints

1 Underestimating their investment time horizon.

As mentioned previously, an investor's time horizon is the period from the present to the future point in time when the investor will no longer need the assets in his or her portfolio. Two examples of why an investor will no longer need his or her assets include having more assets than needed to cover his or her everyday expenses or the death of the investor. Many investors mistakenly estimate their time horizon is from the present to the day they plan to retire. Unfortunately that could not be further from the truth. At retirement, it is not their time horizon that changes, but rather their risk tolerance and liquidity needs that change.

2 Not determining or inaccurately determining their specific financial goals.

You cannot hit a target you are not aiming for. Without a solid understanding of your specific financial goals, you will not be able to manage your portfolio properly. Since your risk tolerance is based partially on your specific financial goals, an accurate assessment is essential to establish your optimal asset mix.

If you don't know where you're going, you'll end up somewhere else.

– Yogi Berra

3 Miscalculating their level of risk tolerance.

Investors often miscalculate either their willingness or ability to assume risk. If you miscalculate your risk tolerance, then you will either have a portfolio that inherently has more risk than appropriate or you may have a portfolio where the expected returns will be less than needed because the portfolio was designed to maximize returns based on a lower risk tolerance.

False conclusions which have been reasoned out are indefinitely worse than blind impulse.

– Horace Mann

4 Misjudging their liquidity needs during their time horizon.

Underestimating how much liquidity you need may put you in a situation where you might have to reallocate some of your assets from growth-oriented investments to income-oriented investments, thus incurring costs (transaction and taxes). Consequently, your portfolio's actual results may underperform expected results, especially in the short-term.

5 Not identifying their unique circumstances or preferences.

Investors need to identify their unique circumstances and preferences and incorporate them into the portfolio management process. This is especially true when utilizing the expertise of a portfolio manager. Communicating that you wish to sell your business and retire early at age 52 would be considered highly important and relevant to a portfolio manager.

Chapter 6

Designing & Constructing Your Optimal Portfolio

♦ ♦ ♦

Investment decisions should focus first and foremost on markets or asset classes, over time, that's going to explain roughly ninety percent of investment returns.

– Gary Brinson

Introduction to Designing Your Optimal Portfolio

Once you have established your objectives and constraints, focus is then shifted to designing your optimal portfolio. A properly designed portfolio is one that stands the best chances of achieving your goals within the context of your objectives and constraints. In other words, your goal is to design a portfolio that maximizes your portfolio's expected total rate of return given the level of risk you are willing and able to assume, all while adhering to your constraints. To accomplish this goal, you will first need to identify your optimal asset mix. Accomplishing this task is not easy and requires many steps. Your optimal asset mix is based on the risk and return trade-off profile most appropriate for your situation.

The first step in identifying your optimal asset mix is to decide which asset classes and asset subclasses to employ. This decision is defined by the inherent risk and return trade-off profile of each asset class and asset subclass. A good rule of thumb is to use the primary asset classes (i.e. equities, fixed-income, cash & equivalents, and alternative assets) and some of the asset subclasses, namely growth and value, domestic and international and large cap and small cap.

Once appropriate asset classes and asset subclasses have been selected, you will then establish the percentage weightings for each within your portfolio. This decision not only establishes your initial weightings, but also guides rebalancing efforts. If and when rebalancing actions are initiated, your optimal asset mix serves as the point where over or under extended asset allocations are returned.

Your optimal asset mix should be established to deliver a specific risk and return trade-off profile. As we know, the appropriate risk and return trade-off profile is based on your objectives and constraints. For example, a moderate risk tolerant investor may have 60% in equity securities, 25% in fixed-income securities, 10% in cash & equivalents and 5% in alternative assets. Moreover, an aggressive risk tolerant investor may have 85% in equity securities, 5% in fixed-income securities, 5% in cash & equivalents and 5% in alternative assets. Take for example the same moderate risk tolerant investor from above who has a much shorter investment time horizon. Given this scenario, the investor will want to allocate fewer assets to equities and more to fixed-income and cash & equivalents. As a result, his or her portfolio may comprise 40%

equities, 35% fixed-income, 25% cash & equivalents, and no alternative assets.

Portfolio managers who specialize in asset allocation usually have model portfolios with established optimal asset mixes. Depending on your appropriate risk and return trade-off profile, portfolio managers will allocate your assets to match one of their model portfolios, thus establishing your optimal asset mix. Appendix A of this book provides a risk tolerance worksheet and suggests a target asset mix based on your responses to the questions posed.

FIGURE 6.1

Sample Optimal Asset Mix Models

Investor's Risk Tolerance	Equities	Fixed-income	Cash & Equivalents	Alternative Assets
Low	25%	50%	25%	0%
Low to Moderate	40	40	20	0
Moderate	55	30	10	5
Moderate to High	70	20	5	5
High	80	5	5	10

Allocation range

Since rebalancing a portfolio is not feasible every time an asset class weighting deviates from its optimal weighting, allocation ranges need to be established. Allocation ranges define the acceptable range that asset allocation weightings are allowed to move within without triggering rebalancing.

Allocation ranges are not necessarily the same for every investor. Rather, they can be narrow, moderate or wide depending on the desired degree of discipline. For instance, if your equity optimal asset mix were established at 60%, the allocation range for equities could be 50-70% for a low discipline approach or 55-65% for a high discipline approach. There is no harden rule for how much flexibility to incorporate. However, a good way to approach this decision is to establish a discipline in correlation to your risk tolerance while taking into consideration your ability and willingness to initiate rebalancing actions. Thus, if you wish to be more aggressive, then you can incorporate more flexibility to your allocation ranges, thus establishing wider ranges. Conversely, if you wish to be less aggressive, then you can incorporate less flexibility. As a result, your allocation ranges will be much more narrow.

Liquidity

There are times when investors with the same risk tolerance have different liquidity needs. As a result, you will need to address this by allocating a greater or lesser amount of each asset class to income-oriented investments or those with higher interest and dividend yields. If two investors have identical risk tolerances, but different liquidity needs, then simply changing their optimal asset mixes to address this difference is not appropriate. More accurately, the securities within each asset class or asset subclass should be changed. For example, the optimal asset mix of an investor with a higher need for liquidity should not be modified to allow for fewer equities and more fixed-income securities. Rather, the equity and fixed-income investments should be selected to provide a higher dividend yield than the equity and fixed-income investments of the investor with a lower liquidity need. Remember, changing your optimal asset mix will change the risk and return trade-off profile of your portfolio.

Management style

There are two styles in which you can manage your portfolio's assets. The first is called passive management and the second is called active management.

Passive management emphasizes index investments (index funds and exchange-traded funds).

Index Funds

A mutual fund that is managed in such a way as to match its return to that of a specific underlying index, such as the S&P 500 or Dow Jones Industrials Average.

Exchange Traded Funds (ETFs)

A closed-end mutual fund that is managed in such a way as to match its return to that of a specific underlying index, such as the S&P 500 or Dow Jones Industrials Average. ETFs trade on a stock exchange rather than issued by traditional mutual fund companies as do index funds.

The aim of passive management is to design a well-diversified portfolio quickly and easily without attempting to outperform the market via security selection. Over the last few years, there has been a proliferation in the number of index investments available to the individual investor. The advantage of index investments is that they provide a quick and easy way to build a well-diversified portfolio at reasonable costs. Most index investments have management fees under 0.75%. The same cannot be said for actively managed funds.

Active management on the other hand attempts to beat the market by employing security selection and market timing. As we know, security selection and market timing do explain a portion of investment performance, but only marginally. By employing active management, you are betting that you or your portfolio manager has the skills and talents to beat the market consistently. Lastly, since active management requires greater resources to employ, you must pay to play, so to speak.

Investment style

Investment style addresses how you should allocate your equity assets between growth and value securities. Investment style is a method whereby you can enhance your equity asset class return while at the same time reducing risk. Does this sound familiar? Hopefully it does. A good way to think of investment style is asset allocation for equity securities. Growth stocks and value stocks are asset subclasses of the equity asset class.

The vast majority of equity securities can be classified as either growth stocks or value stocks. As with asset classes, the securities in each group tend to move together. Thus, when one growth stock is performing strongly, so to do other growth stocks for the most part. This isn't always the case, but there is a solid positive correlation among the stocks in the group. The same goes for value stocks as well.

So why is this so important? Going back to the fundamentals of asset allocation, investments that are not perfectly positively correlated, provide the benefit of increased return and reduced risk. Since growth and value stocks have a low correlation, including both equity asset subclasses in your portfolio is very desirable.

FIGURE 6.2

Benefit of Adding Growth and Value Stocks to a Portfolio

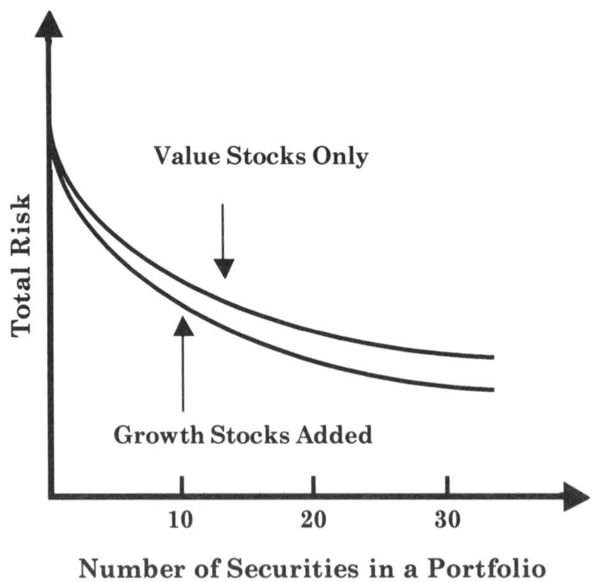

Market capitalization style

Similar to investment style, market capitalization style can also be viewed as asset allocation within the equity asset class. As with value and growth stocks, the stocks within each market capitalization group (small, middle and large) tend to move together. At times, small 'cap' stocks will show signs of strength while at other times large 'cap' stocks will show signs of strength. To capture the correlation benefits of market capitalization, you should allocate a portion of your equity investments to the three capitalizations. Note that there is a fourth market capitalization asset subclass called micro caps, however, given this subclasses' significant risk level and lack of proper investing methods, I have omitted the subclass from this book. In practice, the larger the market capitalization the less price volatility and therefore the lower return potential it has. As a result, less risk tolerant investors should emphasize larger market capitalization stocks over small and middle market capitalization stocks.

FIGURE 6.3

Benefit of Adding Different Capitalizations to a Portfolio

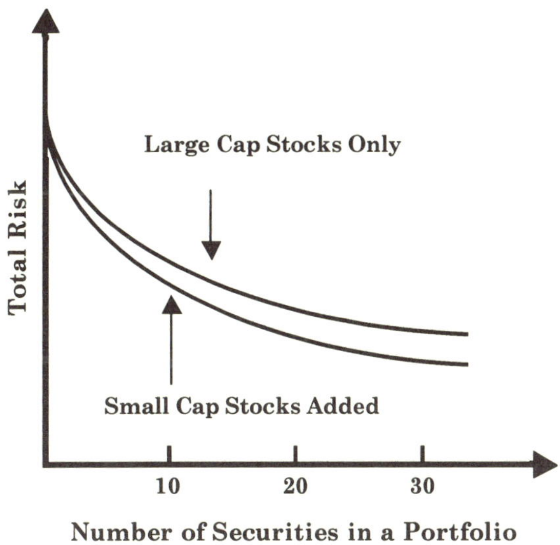

International emphasis

By including international assets to your investment portfolio, you add a new level of sophistication to your risk and return trade-off profile. At the same time, you are also able to enhance the expected return of your portfolio while decreasing risk. Why? The reason is because international assets have less than perfect correlations with domestic assets. As you know, less than perfectly positively correlated assets provide much desired benefits to the risk and return trade-off profile of your portfolio.

FIGURE 6.4

Benefits of Adding International Assets

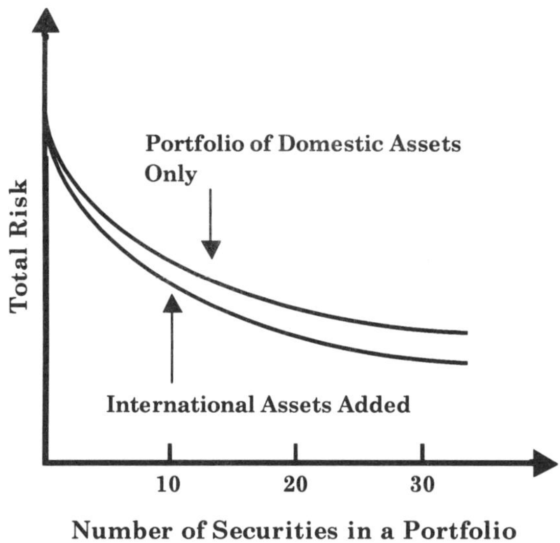

International assets can be found in each asset class, including practically all of the asset subclasses as well. Since evaluating and selecting international assets is more difficult than with domestic assets, investing in international assets is not always appropriate. For the investor who relies upon a professional investment advisor, investing in international assets should be highly considered. Otherwise, investors may want to de-emphasize them. For those investors comfortable with international investments, purchasing shares of an index investment may be the most convenient and appropriate method of investing internationally. Please see chapter nine as it discusses the benefits, costs and risks of global asset allocation.

FIGURE 6.5

Benefits of Adding Multiple Asset Subclasses to a Portfolio

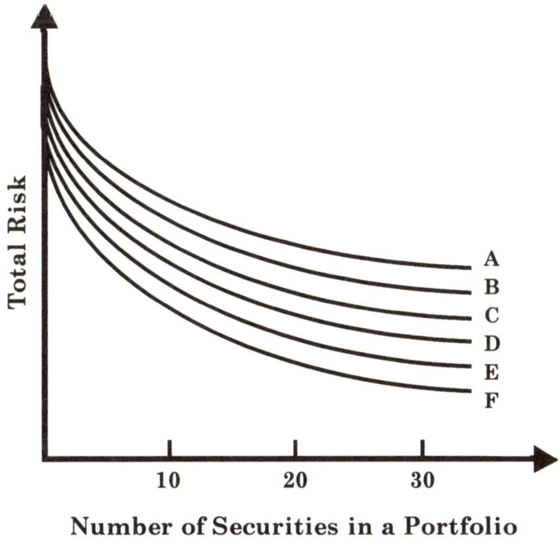

A: Portfolio of domestic large cap value stocks
B: International large cap value stocks added
C: Domestic large cap growth stocks added
D: Domestic small cap value stocks added
E: International large cap growth stocks added
F: Domestic small cap growth stocks added

Portfolio construction

There are four primary methods to construct your optimal portfolio.

These four methods include:

- Individual securities
- Separately managed accounts
- Mutual funds
- Index investments

Deciding which construction method to use is vastly less important than deciding which asset classes and asset subclasses to employ. Consider for example someone planning a vacation. The hard part is deciding where, when, and how. Once this is decided, actually going on the vacation is much easier. Depending on how you will address the aforementioned concepts, specifically management style, the decision of which construction method to employ could be more or less already made. A decision to employ passive management will automatically eliminate individual securities, separately managed accounts and actively managed mutual funds from the equation.

Each of the construction methods has their own advantages and disadvantages. Individual stocks provide the best way to take advantage of security selection. Stocks can be screened and selected based on your judgment or the judgment of your portfolio manager. Unfortunately, this advantage is also a disadvantage if executed poorly. If the screens used or assumptions made regarding the expected returns of the securities are inaccurate, then the portfolio could perform poorly. If you decide to pursue this method you may want to consider implementing a security selection system or method, such as the dogs of the Dow system or programs offered by Value Line and Standard and Poors.

Separately managed accounts, also commonly referred to as wrap accounts, have become very popular over the last few years. With separately managed accounts, an external portfolio manager manages either your entire portfolio or a select part of it. Unlike mutual funds, separately managed accounts allow for more customized portfolios since the portfolio manager has first hand knowledge of your objectives and constraints. Moreover, with separately managed accounts the portfolio manager can tailor his management to your needs rather than the needs of thousands of investors, as mutual fund portfolio managers must do. The principal drawback to separately managed accounts is their higher fees. Higher fees are necessary to compensate for the specialized and customized management. Another drawback to separately managed accounts is their high initial minimums, typically around $100,000. Lastly, just because a portfolio is managed by a separate and external portfolio manager does not mean your portfolio will gain a performance advantage over other portfolios. Sometimes the performance of separately managed accounts will surpass the market and sometimes not. The performance depends on the skills of the portfolio manager. A little luck doesn't hurt either.

Mutual funds provide many advantages, but also come with many disadvantages. Mutual funds provide professional management similar to separately managed accounts. Mutual funds biggest advantages are their low minimums, significant liquidity and means to easily and quickly build a well-diversified portfolio. Most mutual funds have small initial minimum investments, many around $1,000.

The biggest disadvantages of mutual funds are their high expenses, sometimes approaching 1.4% for equity mutual funds, and the excessive turnover of securities, which creates capital gain events for you. It is not uncommon for some aggressive mutual funds to turnover close to 90% of their holdings each year. Talk about little to no focus on tax management!

Index investments have also become very popular over the last several years. Index investments provide the means for you to manage your portfolio passively. Most investors are gravitating to index investments as a way to reduce volatility in their investment portfolios.

Index investments provide two important advantages. First and most obvious, they provide for a well-diversified portfolio. Index investments usually represent, or track, a market of some kind. For example, some index investments represent the market as a whole, such as the S&P 500, or represent specific industry groups, such as financials, pharmaceuticals, software and semiconductors. With index investments, there is no need to worry about security selection as they represent all of the securities within that group. The second advantage with index investments is their low annual management fees. Depending on the market an index investment tracks and to some degree the index investment sponsor, an index investment can have an annual management fee as low as ¼%. That's four to six times lower than the management fees of most actively managed mutual funds.

The biggest disadvantage of index investments is their lack of ability to beat the market. Since they represent the market, by definition they cannot beat the market. This may be an issue with some investors, but successful investors realize that investing is not about swinging for the fences on every pitch.

FIGURE 6.6

Select Exchange-Traded Funds Available for Investment

Exchange Traded Fund *	Symbol
Equities - Domestic	
Dow Jones U.S. Total Market	IYY
S&P 500	IVV
S&P 400 MidCap 400	IJF
S&P 600 SmallCap 600	IJR
Russell 1000 Value	IWB
Russell 1000 Growth	IWF
Equities – International	
S&P Global 100	IOO
S&P Europe 350	IEV
MSCI EAFE Index Fund	EFA

Fixed Income	
GS Corporate Bond Fund	LQD
Lehman 1-3 Year Treasury Bond Fund	SHY
Lehman 7-10 Year Treasury Bond Fund	IEF
Lehman 20+ Year Treasury Bond Fund	TLT
Alternatives	
Dow Jones U.S. Real Estate Fund	IYR
Cohen & Steers Realty Majors Fund	ICF

* From the iShare program advised by Barclays Global Investments.

As a rule of thumb, investors with small portfolios should employ mutual funds and those with larger portfolios should consider either individual securities or separately managed accounts. Index investments work well with any investor. Aside from using portfolio size to determine which construction method to employ, it is simply a matter of personal preference.

Tax management

Since taxes on both capital gains and on interest and dividends can have such a drastic impact on the performance of your portfolio, it is necessary to define how you should approach this issue. The primary questions with tax management are:

- Is your portfolio tax-exempt?
- What is your federal tax rate?

If your portfolio is tax-exempt, then tax management is more or less irrelevant. However, if your portfolio is not tax-exempt, then you need to place emphasis on tax management issues. Depending on your federal tax rate, the focus might call for more tax-exempt fixed-income securities or more corporate fixed-income securities. In practice, investors with taxable portfolios and high federal tax rates should emphasize tax-exempt fixed-income securities, such as municipal bonds and government agency notes. Doing so will increase what is called the tax-equivalent yield.

Tax-Equivalent Yield

The yield you would receive given your tax rate if the income from your fixed-income security were taxable.

Tax-equivalent yield can be defined as the yield you would receive given your tax rate if the income from your fixed-income security were taxable. Since in most cases you do not pay taxes on the interest from tax-exempt securities, your after-tax return is thus higher. Investors with lower tax brackets should consider taxable fixed-income securities since the tax bite will not be large enough to justify a lower yielding tax-exempt security.

With capital gains, it is very important to consider the impact of taxes on the performance of your portfolio. Since asset allocation calls for investments in asset classes and different asset subclasses and not in select securities, you have the ability to offset capital gains by selling some securities with capital losses within the same asset class and then purchasing similar securities in the same asset class to replace them. The IRS frowns upon selling securities strictly to realize a capital loss and buying back nearly identical securities. For example, the capital loss you realize from selling an S&P 500 index may be disallowed by the IRS if you turn around and reinvest the proceeds of the sale within 30 days in the Dow Jones Industrials Average index. These two securities are nearly identical in the eyes of the IRS.

A government which robs Peter to pay Paul can always count on Paul's support.

– George Bernard Shaw

Asset allocation strategy

The question isn't if, but when, you will need to reallocate your assets. Reallocating is another term for rebalancing. Given constantly changing security prices, your portfolio's asset mix will change and, over time, the weightings will begin to stray from your optimal asset mix.

The two strategies commonly employed are strategic asset allocation and tactical asset allocation. A good way to think about strategic asset allocation is to think of it as promoting a fixed asset mix. When employing strategic asset allocation, you should consider rebalancing your portfolio when an asset class weighting moves outside of its allocation range. As mentioned earlier in the chapter, your allocation range depends on the degree of discipline, or flexibility, you wish to bring to the rebalancing process. Only under specific situations will your optimal asset mix change when employing strategic asset allocation.

Tactical asset allocation, on the other hand, allows for changes to your optimal asset mix and allocation ranges in the hope of capturing short-term profit. As an indirect market timing strategy, tactical asset allocation and its benefits need to be considered carefully against its costs (i.e. time and money).

In most circumstances I advocate employing strategic asset allocation unless there is a very good reason to employ tactical asset allocation.

> *An investment operation is one which upon thorough analysis promises safety of principal and an adequate return. Operations not meeting these requirements are speculative.*
>
> – Benjamin Graham

How To Design Your Optimal Portfolio

The following six steps provide a framework for designing your optimal portfolio:

Step 1

Determine your optimal asset mix. Your optimal asset mix is based on your desired risk and return trade-off profile. To identify your profile, you will need to determine the level of risk you are willing and able to assume. A risk tolerance questionnaire may be the best way for you to determine your risk tolerance. A sound risk tolerance questionnaire will evaluate both your willingness and ability (or capacity) to tolerate risk. Appendix A of this book provides such a questionnaire.

- Determine which asset classes to employ.
- Determine how much to allocate to growth and value stocks.
- Determine how much to allocate to small, mid, and large market capitalization stocks.
- Determine the amount, if any, within each asset class you will allocate to international assets.
- Determine how much to allocate within each asset class or asset subclass to match liquidity needs.
- Determine how much to allocate to tax-exempt, if at all, and taxable securities.

Step 2

Establish your allocation ranges, or the acceptable range the percentage weighting of each asset class is permitted to move within without triggering re-balancing. Depending on the degree of discipline you wish to bring to the process, your allocation ranges can be narrow, moderate or wide.

Step 3

Determine whether your portfolio will be actively managed or passively managed.

Step 4

Identify which construction method or methods to employ. The primary methods include individual securities, separately management accounts, mutual funds and index investments. Your portfolio can be a combination of all methods if you so desire.

Step 5

Select your specific investments.

Step 6

Select your asset allocation strategy. Your options include either strategic or tactical.

The above steps have been tailored to the individual investor. However, the steps for institutions are quite similar. Their steps would include an extensive review and forecast of the capital markets going forward. This step was not included for individual investors because of the time, resources and abilities that go into making capital market forecasts. The best solution for you is to use a worksheet, such as the Optimal Allocator provided in Appendix A, to determine yours.

The 8 Biggest Mistakes Investors Make When Designing Their Optimal Portfolios

1 Omitting appropriate asset classes and asset subclasses.

To build their optimal portfolios, investors need to consider all appropriate asset classes and asset subclasses. Each asset class and asset subclass provides return enhancing and risk reducing benefits. By not incorporating appropriate classes, a portfolio may not exhibit the desired risk and return trade-off profile. For example, by omitting value securities from the asset mix, an investor will most likely earn a lower return over the long-term and experience greater portfolio volatility.

2 Selecting inappropriate asset class weightings.

By inappropriately over or under weighting asset classes, an investor's portfolio will exhibit a risk and return trade-off profile that is inconsistent with their objectives and constraints. The result of which is either the assumption of greater risk than appropriate or the portfolio under performing what is expected. The likelihood of achieving their specific financial goals may become endangered.

3 Underestimating the impact of inflation.

As an investor's time horizon increases, the more emphasis an investor should place on defending against the negative impact of inflation. Inflation can erode the real value of a portfolio over time even when the portfolio is experiencing positive actual returns. Portfolios with greater allocations to fixed-income and cash & equivalents are more susceptible to this type of risk. Equity securities provide a solid way to defend against the negative impact of inflation. As a general rule, the longer the investment time horizon the greater allocation to equities a portfolio should have.

4 Neglecting the effects of portfolio management expenses.

Portfolio management expenses come in many different shapes and forms. The two most prominent are management fees and transaction costs. Over time, the compounding effect of portfolio management expenses can be quite large and surprising. Obviously it is more or less impossible not to pay some sort of portfolio related expenses. Nevertheless, you should focus on keeping them as low as possible.

Beware of little expenses; a small leak will sink a great ship.

– Benjamin Franklin

5 Making inaccurate asset class expected total rates of return forecasts.

Estimating asset class expected total rates of return is one of the most difficult tasks associated with designing an optimal portfolio. The best solution for individual investors is to use historical asset class returns rather than attempting to forecast them. A good portfolio manager will have incorporated either historical returns or appropriate forecasts into their asset allocation model rendering this task irrelevant to the individual investor.

6 Overestimating the level of diversification within their portfolio.

Diversification is key to reducing risk, specifically security-specific risk. There are two ways an investor may overestimate the level of diversification. First, they may believe the quantity of securities currently in their portfolio is sufficient to create a diversified portfolio when, in fact, it is not. Second, but much less important, although an investor may purchase the appropriate quantity of securities, the majority of these may be too similar to provide significant diversification benefits. For example, purchasing General Motors and Ford will provide some diversification benefits, but due to their inherent similarities, they will not provide the level of diversification an investor needs.

7 Miscalculating the impact of taxes.

Many times investors will let the impact of taxes impede their decisions to sell investments. It is true that taxes do sometimes take a big chunk of profits, however, investors need to base their decisions on whether the investment is suitable and appropriate. On the other hand, there are a number of investors who do place to little emphasis on the impact of taxes. Turnover and the resulting capital gains can wreak havoc on a portfolio's performance. In summary, investors need to balance tax considerations with investment considerations.

8 Confusing diversification with asset allocation.

The first thing that usually comes to mind when an investor hears of asset allocation is the concept of diversification. They then incorrectly assume that their diversified portfolio has been allocated properly. This cannot be further from the truth. Diversification only deals with the management of risk, specifically the reduction of company-specific risk. On the other hand, asset allocation not only maximizes return given the risk tolerance of the investor, but also reduces risk by combining asset classes that have less than perfect correlations. Said another way, asset allocation deals with both the numerator and denominator of the risk and return trade-off equation while diversification only deals with the numerator.

Constructing Your Optimal Portfolio

This phase of the portfolio management process entails implementing the designed financial plan outlined in the Investment Policy Statement to build your desired optimal portfolio. The construction of your optimal portfolio is rather straightforward since the vast majority of your decisions have already been made during the design phase. The process of constructing an optimal portfolio is much like the processes of building a house or assembling a bookshelf, whereas you simply need to read the instructions and follow the directions.

Of the four phases of portfolio management, the construction phase is the least time consuming. The most difficult part of this phase is selecting investments that will comprise your portfolio and to select them within the context of the decisions you answered during the design stage, such as whether to use active management or passive management and how much emphasis to place on international investments. Your job becomes even easier if you have decided to use index investments or mutual funds. Only when you have decided to use individual securities does your job of constructing your optimal portfolio become more time consuming.

Aside from simply implementing the plan as designed in the previous phase, your significant task in the construction phase is to select a financial services firm to execute your transactions and hold your portfolio. You have many available choices from full-service firms to discount firms. Given the elimination of the Glass-Steagall Act of 1933, insurance companies and banks have entered the investment business with force and provide you with more options.

How to Construct Your Optimal Portfolio

The following three steps provide a framework for constructing your optimal portfolio:

Step 1

Review and understand your Investment Policy Statement. Everything you need to implement should be contained within this document.

Step 2

Select a financial services firm (Ameritrade, Fidelity, Charles Schwab, Merrill Lynch, etc) that provides the services you desire at reasonable costs. Many investors may want to seek professional help rather than to implement their plan by themselves. Chapter thirteen of this book provides some insights into obtaining professional counsel as well as a list of questions to ask when evaluating an advisor. Although not always the case, the decision of which financial services firm to use has already been made and outlined in your Investment Policy Statement.

Step 3

Implement the plan as outlined in your Investment Policy Statement.

The 3 Biggest Mistakes Investors Make When Constructing Their Optimal Portfolios

1 Selecting an inappropriate financial services firm.

When it comes time to select a financial services firm, an investor needs to carefully consider what services they require and how much the financial services firm will charge. For investors looking for a little extra help and professional guidance, a full-service firm is appropriate. Most discount financial services firms do not provide advice as well as some of the high-end services. On the other hand, for those do-it-yourselfers, discount financial services firms may be more appropriate. Given the increased costs associated with doing business with a full-service firm, you need to consider what services you really need so you do not end up paying a premium for services not suitable to your situation. Also, you could run into the problem of having a financial advisor at a full-service firm attempt to change the plan as outlined in your Investment Policy Statement. Some, but not all, of these guys will even try and sell you on security selection over asset allocation. Many of my CPA friends tell me how they create financial plans for their clients only to have those plans completely revised by investment advisors. Keep a watchful eye.

2 Not implementing the guidelines as set forth in the Investment Policy Statement.

Your IPS was created to help you achieve your specific financial goals. By not following the plan, you throw everything you have worked on out the window and leave everything to chance. You can't hit a target with your eyes closed.

3 Taking too long to implement.

The time for moving slowly is during the design phase, not the construction phase. Once you have designed your optimal portfolio and drafted your Investment Policy Statement, the execution of your plan should proceed swiftly. Your time horizon is already on the clock so to speak, and so to should your portfolio.

Chapter 7

Drafting Your Investment Policy Statement

♦ ♦ ♦

Importance of the Investment Policy Statement

Much like a blueprint for building a house, an Investment Policy Statement serves as a blueprint for building your optimal portfolio. This policy is crucial to the long-term achievement of your specific financial goals. First and foremost, an Investment Policy Statement helps you to learn more about what your needs and priorities are, how to best address them, and the risks involved with investing. Secondly, this policy allows you and your portfolio manager (if you elect to employ one) to gain a better understanding of your objectives and constraints and how to best manage your portfolio to accomplish your specific financial goals. Without an Investment Policy Statement, a portfolio manager may make inappropriate investment decisions such as incorporating high risk asset classes in an otherwise conservative to moderate risk portfolio or incorporating more fixed-income asset classes in a growth-oriented portfolio. This could result in a portfolio that underachieves its intended purpose or incorporates greater risk than appropriate.

A written Investment Policy Statement will not alone guarantee success in protecting and growing your optimal portfolio. Rather, it will shelter your portfolio from ad hoc revisions, made by either you or your portfolio manager, from a sound long-term asset allocation policy.

Outline of an Investment Policy Statement

A properly drafted Investment Policy Statement outlines the asset classes and asset subclasses selected for investment and their respective weightings within your portfolio. In addition, many policies also make mention of security selection and timing strategies. A properly drafted Investment Policy Statement clearly articulates your objectives and constraints as well as how to address and incorporate them within the portfolio management process.

Your IPS should make every effort to incorporate the following:

- Your current portfolio
- Your objectives and constraints
- Recommended (or desired) portfolio
- Portfolio construction process
- Portfolio monitoring process
- Portfolio rebalancing process
- Annual review process
- Agreement between you and your portfolio manager

Benefits of an Investment Policy Statement

Articulating your specific financial goals and objectives and constraints provides a benchmark, or objective standard, with which to evaluate your portfolio manager. For example, clearly specifying in the Investment Policy Statement which asset classes or asset subclasses to incorporate will allow for the selection of an appropriate benchmark, such as the S&P 500, Wilshire 5000, or Goldman Sachs Corporate Bond Fund. A portfolio comprising low risk asset classes should be compared against low risk benchmarks, while portfolios with high risk asset classes should be compared against high risk benchmarks. Once the benchmark or benchmarks are selected, you will be able to compare the performance of your portfolio manager against the index or indices, or alternatively what you could earn through passive, rather than active, portfolio management. The greater the positive deviation between the return of your portfolio and the return of the appropriate benchmark, the more value your portfolio manager has added. Conversely, the greater the negative deviation the more value the portfolio manager has destroyed. In that scenario we all know what usually results; time for a new portfolio manager.

An Investment Policy Statement also helps to curb unethical behaviour on the part of your portfolio manager. Given that your objectives and constraints are clearly spelled out in written form for all interested parties, miscommunications or actions such as “playing the market” or taking unnecessary chances, are not only easier to discover, but also much less likely to occur.

Another significant benefit of using an Investment Policy Statement is when there is a change in portfolio managers. Due to many reasons, both occurring within the investment firm and with the portfolio manager, most portfolio managers will manage your portfolio for only a couple of years, possibly five at best. Since your time horizon may extend out twenty or more years, one can easily visualize the large number of portfolio managers you may have. As a result, an Investment Policy Statement will ensure a smooth transition from portfolio manager to portfolio manager. The new portfolio manager will be able to jump right in where the previous portfolio manager left off, thus reducing any potential delays in monitoring and rebalancing your portfolio and promoting consistency of management.

The Investment Policy Statement may take many forms, from simple asset class targets to highly complex and often times specific criteria. Some policy statements may even state which investments a portfolio manager is prohibited from incorporating, such as real estate, commodities, derivatives or foreign bonds. The written IPS will assist you to maintain a long-term approach when short-term market volatility may bring about stressful nights and misgivings about the plan. In the past, only institutional clients had utilized Investment Policy Statements. However, due to its many benefits, utilizing an IPS is now common for individuals as well.

Summary of Benefits

- Assists you to more fully understand what your specific financial goals are and how best to prioritize them.
- Assists the portfolio manager to understand what your objectives and constraints are and how to best manage your portfolio.
- Outlines your optimal asset mix, asset allocation strategy, and construction method (sometimes including security selection and timing).
- Establishes what management style, investment style, and market capitalization style your portfolio manager must employ.
- Provides a benchmark or benchmarks with which to evaluate the performance of your portfolio manager.
- Guards the portfolio against making ad hoc decisions that will impede your long-term strategy.

- Greatly decreases miscommunications and misunderstandings and allows for such occurrences to be quickly and easily resolved.

Updating Your Investment Policy Statement

An Investment Policy Statement should be reviewed and, if appropriate, modified at least annually. A comprehensive review of your return aspirations, risk tolerance, liquidity needs, time horizon, legal considerations, and unique circumstances & preferences should be made and any changes incorporated into the existing policy. It is your responsibility to communicate to your portfolio manager any and all changes to your financial situation as soon as possible. Doing so will help your portfolio manager work towards achieving your specific financial goals and objectives.

How to Draft Your Investment Policy Statement

The following eleven steps provide a framework for drafting your Investment Policy Statement:

Step 1

Collect all essential financial documents, including your latest monthly investment statement, the objectives and constraints you identified in chapter five and the portfolio you designed in chapter six.

Step 2

Write the purpose of the IPS so that all interested parties know why you are using it.

Step 3

Develop and write an executive summary, including your objectives and constraints and key points addressed in the design of your optimal portfolio.

Step 4

Summarize your current portfolio.

Step 5

Outline the optimal portfolio you designed in the previous chapter. Here is where you include the asset classes and asset subclasses you will employ. In addition, you should include the percentage weightings for each, along with allocation range ceilings and floors.

Step 6

Outline how the portfolio manager shall construct your optimal portfolio. Your options include individual securities, separately managed accounts (wrap accounts, hedge funds and related), mutual funds and index investments.

Step 7

Outline how the portfolio manager shall monitor your optimal portfolio. Here you could list the benchmark or benchmarks you will evaluate performance against.

Step 8

Outline how the portfolio manager shall rebalance your optimal portfolio.

Step 9

Communicate the duties and responsibilities of the portfolio manager and yourself (feel free to use the ones from the following IPS example).

Step 10

Define the annual review procedures (again feel free to use the procedures from the following IPS).

Step 11

Obtain a signature from the appropriate person at the investment firm and sign the document yourself.

The 5 Biggest Mistakes Investors Make With Their Investment Policy Statements

1 Leave out critical information.

The success of the Investment Policy Statement is dependent on how complete and accurate it is. By not communicating some important piece of information, the portfolio manager will have to fill in the blank. Leave nothing to chance.

2 Draft the IPS too vague and ambiguous.

Although the IPS may include all of the critical information, it does no good if the quality of the information is suspect. Be clear and concise in your writing.

3 Fail to have their portfolio manager review and understand their IPS.

The Investment Policy Statement is only as good as how closely it is followed. Most of the top portfolio managers will have their own in-house Investment Policy Statements and therefore understand its importance. Otherwise, make a concerted effort to have your portfolio manager review your IPS and communicate that he or she is on the same page as you.

4 Fail to monitor the compliance of their portfolio manager.

Even with the best intentions, a portfolio manager may not fully comply with the guidelines as set forth in the IPS. Therefore, investors should monitor their portfolio to ensure that all actions taken are suitable and appropriate.

5 Fail to revise their IPS as needed.

Over time, an investor's objectives and constraints as well as his or her specific financial goals will most likely change. As a result, the investor or portfolio manager needs to revise the investor's Investment Policy Statement to address these changes. As a general rule, an IPS should be evaluated and possibly revised annually. The benefits of using an IPS are dependent on its accuracy.

SAMPLE
INVESTMENT POLICY STATEMENT

INVESTMENT POLICY STATEMENT

Prepared for

John & Mary Smart

As of

May 2003

Frush Financial Group

Bloomfield Hills, Michigan

Purpose of this Investment Policy Statement

An Investment Policy Statement (IPS) provides the foundation for the investment management of your portfolio. This document will guide you and your portfolio manager through the portfolio management process ensuring that decision-making will be executed within the context of your objectives and constraints even when unexpected market fluctuations would otherwise tempt short-term deviations.

This document establishes the criteria against which the portfolio's performance will be monitored, evaluated and measured.

The final goal of an Investment Policy Statement is to promote a valuable exchange of communication between you and your portfolio manager.

Executive Summary

Account Title:	John and Mary Smart	**SSN:**	123-45-6789 & 234-56-7890
Custodian:	Ameritrade	**Accountant:**	Tami Smith, CPA
Legal Counsel:	Brent Jones	**Insurance Agent:**	Barbara Brown

OBJECTIVES & CONSTRAINTS

OBJECTIVES

Return Aspiration:

▼

LOW	MODERATE	HIGH

Risk Tolerance:

▼

LOW MODERATE HIGH

CONSTRAINTS

Time Horizon:

▼

SHORT MODERATE LONG

Liquidity Needs:

▼

LOW MODERATE HIGH

Tax Considerations:

▼

FEW MODERATE NUMEROUS

Legal & Regulatory Considerations:

▼

FEW MODERATE NUMEROUS

Unique Circumstances & Preferences:

▼

FEW MODERATE NUMEROUS

DESIGN GUIDELINES AND PROVISIONS

Portfolio Trade-Off Profile

▼

CAP PRESERVATION BALANCED CAP APPRECIATION

Allocation Range Discipline

LOW | MODERATE | HIGH

Liquidity

INCOME-ORIENTED | BALANCED | GROWTH-ORIENTED

Management Style

PASSIVE | BLEND | ACTIVE

Investment Style

VALUE | BLEND | GROWTH

Market Capitalization Style

SMALL CAP | MID CAP | LARGE CAP

International Emphasis

LOW | MODERATE | HIGH

Construction Method

INDIVIDUAL SEC | SEP MANAGED | MUTUAL FUNDS | INDEXING

Tax Management Focus

TAX-EXEMPT	LOW	MODERATE	▼ HIGH

Asset Allocation Strategy

▼ STRATEGIC	INTEGRATED	TACTICAL

CURRENT PORTFOLIO

Total Market Value: $1,524,000

Asset Allocation	
Equities	
U.S.	50%
International	5
Fixed-income	
U.S.	25
International	0
Cash & equivalents	15
Alternatives	
Commodities	0
Real Estate	0

RECOMMENDED PORTFOLIO

Asset Class	Lower Limit	Optimal Asset Mix	Upper Limit
Equities			
U.S.	40%	45%	50%
International	10	15	20
Fixed-income			
U.S.	15	20	25
International	3	5	7
Cash & equivalents	7	10	13
Alternatives			
Commodities	0	0	0
Real Estate	3	5	7

Portfolio Trade-Off Profile
Defines the appropriate risk and return trade-off profile for the portfolio given your return aspiration and risk tolerance.

Recommended Portfolio Trade-Off Profile:

▼

CAP PRESERVATION	BALANCED	CAP APPRECIATION

Allocation Range Discipline
Defines to what degree your portfolio's asset allocation mix is allowed to deviate from the optimal asset mix before the portfolio manager must rebalance.

Recommended Allocation Range Discipline:

▼

LOW	MODERATE	HIGH

Liquidity Focus
Defines to what degree the assets in your portfolio should emphasize current income (dividends and interest) over capital appreciation (security price appreciation).

Recommended Liquidity Focus:

▼

INCOME-ORIENTED BALANCED GROWTH-ORIENTED

Management Style
Defines whether your portfolio should emphasize active or passive management.

Recommended Management Style:

▼

PASSIVE BLEND ACTIVE

Investment Style
Defines to what degree your portfolio should be comprised of value or growth stocks.

Recommended Investment Style:

▼

VALUE BLEND GROWTH

Market Capitalization Style
Defines to what degree the portfolio should be comprised of small, medium, or large capitalization securities.

Recommended Market Capitalization Style:

▼

SMALL CAP MID CAP LARGE CAP

International Emphasis
Defines to what degree the portfolio should be comprised of international assets.

Recommended International Emphasis:

	▼	
LOW	MODERATE	HIGH

Construction Method
Defines the primary method the portfolio manager should employ when constructing the portfolio.

Recommended Construction Method:

▼			
INDIVIDUAL SEC	SEP MANAGED	MUTUAL FUNDS	INDEXING

Tax Management Focus
Defines what emphasis should be placed on minimizing taxes and maximizing after-tax net returns.

Recommended Tax Management Focus:

		▼	
TAX-EXEMPT	LOW	MODERATE	HIGH

Asset Allocation Strategy
Defines which asset allocation strategy should be employed.

Recommended Asset Allocation Strategy:

▼		
STRATEGIC	INTEGRATED	TACTICAL

CONSTRUCTING YOUR PORTFOLIO

This step provides the framework for how best to construct the portfolio that has been proposed in the previous section. There are four primary construction methods available to employ, as follows:

- Individual securities
- Separately managed accounts
- Mutual funds
- Index investments

A portfolio manager can employ any one or more of the above methods. Thus, a portfolio can be constructed with both individual stocks and mutual funds. Each method presents its own advantages and disadvantages.

MONITORING YOUR PORTFOLIO

Portfolio appraisals and performance reports will be provided to you on a quarterly basis. The performance of the portfolio will be measured against an appropriate benchmark or benchmarks. Given the proposed portfolio and resulting optimal asset mix, the following benchmarks will be employed:

Portfolio Proposed Asset Class	Proposed *Optimal Asset Mix*	Benchmark
Equities		
U.S.	45%	S&P 500
International	15	EAFE
Fixed-income		
U.S.	25	GSCBFI
International	0	N/A
Cash & equivalents	10	N/A
Alternatives		
Commodities	0	N/A
Real Estate	5	Dow REIF

Your portfolio will be reviewed and analyzed at least quarterly. Specific emphasis will be placed on the portfolio's asset allocation mix and then compared against both the optimal asset mix and the allocation ranges. Deviations above or below the respective allocation ranges are grounds for rebalancing.

Rebalancing Your Portfolio

Rebalancing is the process of reallocating asset classes to match the optimal asset mix. Due to price movements, some asset classes will need to be sold while others will need to be purchased. Rebalancing may occur if allocations move outside of allocation ranges. This occurs when asset allocations move above established ceiling levels or allocations move below established floor levels. Lastly, although asset class allocations may be within the allocation range, rebalancing may occur at any time for various reasons if allocations deviate from the optimal asset mix.

Your optimal asset mix is determined primarily by the risk and return trade-off profile desired. Allocation ranges may be modified depending on the asset allocation strategy selected in the design phase.

- **Strategic:** A strategy whereby asset class weightings within a portfolio are fixed. When appropriate, rebalancing is made to return the asset class weightings to the optimal asset mix.
- **Tactical:** An indirect market timing strategy whereby a portfolio manager changes the then current optimal asset mix and allocation ranges in response to fluctuating market conditions in the hope of profiting from short-term price movements.
- **Integrated:** A strategy whereby a portfolio manager periodically changes the optimal asset mix and allocation ranges depending on changes to either the investor's objectives and constraints or market conditions. Essentially a combination of strategic and tactical asset allocation strategies.

Annual Review

The client is strongly recommended to review this Investment Policy Statement at least annually and to communicate to Frush Financial Group any and all changes to your:

- Financial situation
- Objectives and constraints

In addition to a review made by the client, Frush Financial Group also agrees to review and evaluate this statement at least annually for feasibility, performance and ability to achieve the client's objectives and constraints.

Agreement

I, ______________________, have completely read, understand, and approve of this Investment Policy Statement. As a result, I authorize the full implementation of this Investment Policy Statement by Frush Financial Group.

Signed this____________ day of_______________, 200___.

_________________________ _________________________

John A. Smart

Scott P. Frush
President, Frush Financial Group

____

Mary T. Smart

Chapter 8

Monitoring & Rebalancing Your Optimal Portfolio

♦ ♦ ♦

There are those who make money in the market and those who keep it.

– Benjamin Graham

Introduction to Monitoring Your Optimal Portfolio

Monitoring is the process of comparing and evaluating your portfolio's asset allocation mix to both your designed optimal asset mix and your asset allocation ranges. In addition, monitoring can also involve comparing and evaluating the portfolio's performance to a benchmark or benchmarks. We will first discuss performance monitoring.

Performance monitoring

Most portfolio managers evaluate the performance of a portfolio on a quarterly basis in order to appease the client. However, evaluating portfolio performance is not as easy as it might initially appear. Why? First, there is the issue of evaluating a portfolio's short-term results when you have designed and implemented a long-term strategy. Only over longer periods of time can the benefits of asset allocation be measured. Any comparisons made using short holding periods are only measuring security selection and market timing, and nothing more. Second, there is difficulty in comparing a multi-class portfolio to a benchmark. Which benchmark or benchmarks do you select? Simply selecting the S&P 500 for a multi-class portfolio will not suffice. The S&P 500 is comprised of equity securities only. Thus, a portfolio comprising fixed-income securities or alternative assets simply would not be appropriate. The solution is to segment each asset class and compare it against an appropriate benchmark, such as the S&P 500 for U.S. equity securities and the EAFE for international equity securities.

An appropriate benchmark[1] to use for comparison purposes should have the following fundamental characteristics:

- **Specified in Advance:** The benchmark should be selected at the time the portfolio is designed.
- **Investable:** The benchmark itself can be purchased.
- **Measurable:** The return of the benchmark can be calculated on a reasonably frequent basis.
- **Appropriate:** The benchmark style is consistent with the style in which your portfolio is managed.
- **Composition Known:** The securities that make up the benchmark are known.
- **Uniform:** The benchmark's time horizon, liquidity, tax management considerations, etc are similar and appropriate to that of the investor.

- **Unambiguous:** The securities and their weightings within the benchmark are representative of the benchmark's style.

[1]Bailey, Jeffery V., CFA, "Are Manager Universes Acceptable Performance Benchmarks?", *The Journal of Portfolio Management*, Spring 1992.

One final thought about performance measurement and monitoring. It is very important to ensure the performance data supplied by your portfolio manager, if you elect to use one, is created using geometric returns rather than arithmetic returns. Why? The reason is because the results can be totally misleading. For instance. Let's say you invest $1,000,000 with a certain portfolio manager. During the following one year, your portfolio suffers a huge loss and is worth $500,000. That's a negative 50% return. The following year your portfolio gains the $500,000 lost in the previous year giving your portfolio a total market value of $1,000,000 at the end of the second year. Thus a return of 100% for year two. Using arithmetic returns, your portfolio manager may claim to have earned you +25% (–50% + 100% divided by 2) during the two-year period. As you can see, your portfolio has not appreciated whatsoever, thus the +25% is not accurate. Using geometric returns, your portfolio manager would report a 0% return rather than a +25% return. This is something to keep in mind.

Asset allocation mix monitoring

A portfolio's asset allocation mix must be compared periodically against your optimal asset mix and allocation ranges. As we know, your optimal asset mix and allocation ranges are established during the design phase. Deviations above or below the allocation range are grounds for rebalancing. Under strategic asset allocation, a portfolio manager may rebalance a portfolio if an asset class weighting were above or below range limits. However, tactical asset allocation is somewhat different. This strategy allows the portfolio manager to alter both the optimal asset mix and allocation ranges in the hope of capturing short-term profits. Consequently, monitoring and rebalancing of your portfolio has as much to do with the strategy selected as it does with your optimal asset mix and allocation ranges established.

How Often Should Monitoring Occur?

The process of monitoring should not be confused with rebalancing. The two concepts do go hand-in-hand, however, only does rebalancing trigger portfolio reallocations.

Monitoring your optimal portfolio is an ongoing process. It should occur at least quarterly, but it could be more appropriate to monitor monthly or even weekly depending on asset class volatility. Rebalancing your portfolio should not occur as frequently however. Decisions to rebalance must be assessed against the costs.

How to Monitor Your Optimal Portfolio

The following six steps provide a framework for monitoring your optimal portfolio. As you will see, the process is rather straightforward and simple.

Step 1

Identify your current portfolio asset class weightings.

Step 2

Compare the current portfolio asset class weightings to your optimal asset mix and allocation ranges.

Step 3

Take notice of any deviations above or below the appropriate allocation range.

Step 4

Evaluate any deviation or deviations within the context of the asset allocation strategy employed (strategic or tactical).

Step 5

Proceed to rebalancing if any deviation or deviations are not appropriate given the asset allocation strategy employed (Note: proceeding to rebalancing does not implicitly mean the weightings in a portfolio must be adjusted since the costs of such an action must be weighed against the benefits).

Step 6

Go to step 1 and repeat the monitoring process.

Introduction to Rebalancing

Rebalancing is the act of reallocating asset classes from current allocation weightings to match your optimal asset mix. Due to asset class price movements (and the resulting change to their weightings in your portfolio), some asset classes will need to be sold while others will need to be purchased. Rebalancing may be triggered if allocations move outside of the allocation range. This occurs when allocations move above established upper limits (ceilings) or allocations move below established lower limits (floors). Upper and lower limits are predicated on the allocation range discipline established during the design phase. Lastly, although asset class allocations may be within the allocation range, rebalancing may occur at any time for various reasons if allocations deviate from your optimal asset mix.

Your optimal asset mix is determined primarily by the risk and return trade-off profile sought by you. Allocation ranges may be modified depending on the asset allocation strategy selected in the design phase. The two strategies include:

- **Strategic:** A strategy whereby you attempt to peg your asset class weightings as close to the weightings as defined by your optimal asset mix. This strategy can be considered a fixed strategy. When appropriate, rebalancing is initiated to return the asset class weightings to their weightings as defined by the optimal asset mix.
- **Tactical:** An active management strategy whereby you change the then-current optimal asset mix and allocation ranges in response to fluctuating market conditions in the hope of profiting from short-term price movements. Current asset weightings are not necessarily changed. Rather, they are allowed to deviate more.

When to Rebalance

As mentioned above, rebalancing may be triggered when a portfolio's asset class weighting moves outside of its previously established allocation range. The important words here are previously established. Why? Because changes in your objectives and constraints or changes to the risk return trade-off profile of asset classes may warrant changes to allocation ranges. Thus, a change to the equity allocation range may cause a portfolio's equity weighting deviate from the allocation range although the equity weighting was within the range before the change. As a result, there are other indirect factors that may or may not trigger rebalancing. Also, under tactical asset allocation, your optimal asset mix and allocation ranges are permitted to change in the hope of profiting from short-term price fluctuations. Thus, the trigger factor is not exactly static with tactical asset allocation.

Some investment advisors advocate rebalancing once per year rather than when asset weightings deviate from their respective allocation ranges. This approach fails to address asset weightings that may have deviated significantly from their optimal asset mix during the year. If someone is going to let his or her asset weighting deviate then there is no reason to place any significant emphasis on determining the optimal asset mix since we know that market forces will change weightings and could do so drastically.

Lastly, you need to consider the possibility that your allocation range discipline, or to what degree your portfolio's asset allocation mix is allowed to deviate from your optimal asset mix before you rebalance, may be too narrow or too wide.

Changes to the Allocation Ranges

There are two principle reasons you or your portfolio manager may need to change a portfolio's allocation ranges. These include changes to your objectives and constraints and changes to asset class risk and return trade-off profiles.

Examples of changes affecting an investor's objectives and constraints

- Specific financial goals
- Wealth
- Risk tolerance
- Time horizon
- Liquidity needs
- Tax considerations
- Legal and regulatory considerations
- Unique circumstances and preferences

Examples of changes affecting asset class risk and return trade-offs

- Asset class return potentials
- Asset class risk potentials
- Macroeconomic factors
- Market portfolio

How Often Should Rebalancing Occur?

Rebalancing your portfolio should occur at least once each year. However, it is prudent to rebalance your portfolio quarterly, and possibly even monthly depending on the degree of volatility in your portfolio. Due to the potential costs involved with rebalancing, it is not appropriate to carry out rebalancing on a weekly basis. To be more specific, the frequency and degree of rebalancing is dependent on the occurrence and degree to which your asset class weightings deviate from both your allocation ranges and optimal asset mix. The wider you set your upper and lower allocation ranges the less frequent you will have to rebalance. Conversely, the tighter the upper and lower allocation ranges, the more frequent you will have to rebalance. On the other hand, although you will have to rebalance less frequently with wider allocation ranges, the amount of rebalancing will be greater.

Costs of Rebalancing

There are two chief costs you need to consider before rebalancing. The first is transaction costs, or the spread between the bid and asking prices and commissions that are charged by a financial services firm to execute a purchase or sell order. Mutual fund loads are considered a transaction cost as well. The second is taxes on potential capital gains from the sale of a security or securities. Depending on the cost basis, capital gains have the potential to dwarf transaction and all other costs associated with executing a sell transaction.

One note of caution - the costs of rebalancing should prompt you to take a short pause, not necessarily stop the process of rebalancing altogether. As mentioned earlier, decisions to sell a security or securities need to be evaluated with respect to their tax implications. However, investment decisions take utmost priority over tax considerations. It is not prudent to cease rebalancing simply to defer capital gains taxes.

Advantages & Disadvantages of Rebalancing

The primary advantage of rebalancing is that your portfolio will continue to exhibit the desired risk and return trade-off profile given your objectives and constraints. As asset classes become more or less pronounced, as a percentage of the total portfolio, the risk and return trade-off profile of your portfolio changes. In order to return the risk and return trade-off profile to equilibrium, rebalancing needs to occur. This task can also be viewed as risk management. Another benefit of rebalancing is that you gain a better sense of how a portfolio operates and how best to manage it.

The primary disadvantage of rebalancing is the cost involved with doing so, as mentioned previously. Also, you need to take into consideration the amount of time required to carry out rebalancing.

How to Rebalance Your Optimal Portfolio

The following seven steps provide a framework for rebalancing your optimal portfolio. These steps assume that you or your portfolio manager has already identified a deviation or deviations outside the allocation range(s) during the monitoring phase and that your asset allocation strategy calls for rebalancing.

Step 1

Determine the amount of rebalancing that is needed. The typical amount is the difference between the current asset weighting and the weighting as defined by your optimal asset mix.

Step 2

Determine the cost basis for any assets that may need to be sold.

Step 3

Determine the costs (transaction and taxes) of selling the asset as determined in step 1.

Step 4

Evaluate whether or not the costs should delay the rebalancing transaction.

Step 5

If the impact of costs does not prove material, either sell or buy the appropriate amount, as determined in step 1.

Step 6

Depending on whether step 5 involved selling or buying, either determine which asset class or classes to sell to fund the purchase or determine which asset class or classes to buy with the proceeds from the asset sold.

Step 7

Reallocate as determined in step 6.

Examples of Rebalancing

Example 1:

Portfolio Specifics:

Asset Class	% Current Weighting	Lower Limit	Optimal Asset Mix	Upper Limit
Equities	55%	30%	40%	50%
Fixed-Income	25%	30%	40%	50%
Cash & Equivalents	20%	15%	20%	25%
Alternatives	---	---	0%	---

Monitoring Observations:

- Equity assets are over their upper limit by 5%, rebalancing may be needed.
- Fixed-income assets are under their lower limit by 5%, rebalancing may be needed.
- Cash & equivalents assets are within their allocation range – no rebalancing is needed.
- No allocation to alternatives.

Rebalancing Actions:

- Sell equity assets in the amount of 15% of the portfolio, which equates to about 27.3% of equity assets.
- Reallocate the proceeds of the sale to fixed-income.

Detailed Description:

The Smith Foundation has an optimal asset mix of 40% equities, 40% fixed-income and 20% cash & equivalents. For allocation ranges, the portfolio has 30%-50% equities, 30%-50% fixed-income, and 15%-25% cash & equivalents. The portfolio employs strategic asset allocation.

Due to a semi-strong equity market and semi-weak fixed-income market, one year later the portfolio's asset mix is comprised of 55% equities, 25% fixed-income, and 20% cash &

equivalents. After evaluating the equity and fixed-income deviations, the portfolio manager decides to move forward with rebalancing. As a result, the portfolio manager sells approximately 27.3% of equities (which represents 15% of the portfolio's total market value) to return the equity weighting to the optimal asset mix. In addition the portfolio manager reallocates the proceeds of the equity sale to fixed-income, thus returning it to the optimal asset mix as well.

Example 2:

Portfolio Specifics:

Asset Class	% Current Weighting	Lower Limit	Optimal Asset Mix	Upper Limit
Equities	63%	45%	55%	65%
Fixed-Income	20%	25%	30%	35%
Cash & Equivalents	10%	7%	10%	13%
Alternatives	7%	3%	5%	7%

Monitoring Observations:

- Equity assets are within their allocation range – no rebalancing is needed.
- Fixed-income assets are under their lower limit by 5%, rebalancing may be needed.
- Cash & equivalents assets are within their allocation range – no rebalancing is needed.
- Alternative assets are within their allocation range – no rebalancing is needed.

Rebalancing Actions:

- Buy 50% more fixed-income assets, which represents 10% of the total portfolio market value.
- Sell a portion of equities and alternatives to fund the purchase of fixed-income securities.

Detailed Description:

The Jones Foundation has an optimal asset mix of 55% equities, 30% fixed-income, 10% cash & equivalents and 5% alternative assets. For allocation ranges, the portfolio has 45%-65% equities, 25%-35% fixed-income, 7%-13% cash & equivalents and 3%-7% alternative assets. The portfolio also employs strategic asset allocation.

Due to strength in equities and alternatives and weakness in fixed-income, one year later the portfolio's asset mix is comprised of 63% equities, 20% fixed-income, 10% cash & equivalents and 7% alternatives. After evaluating the fixed-income deviation, the portfolio manager decides to move forward with rebalancing. As a result, the portfolio manager buys 50% more fixed-income (which represents 10% of the total portfolio market value) to return the fixed-income weighting to the optimal asset mix. In addition, the portfolio manager funds the fixed-income purchase by selling both equities and alternatives. Cash and equivalents asset are not touched in this scenario.

The 4 Biggest Mistakes Investors Make When Monitoring and Rebalancing Their Optimal Portfolios

1 Rebalancing too frequently.

Rebalancing too frequently can expose the investor to higher transaction costs than is appropriate under normal circumstances. In addition, there is the additional time commitment that is needed to rebalance more frequently. As the old saying goes, time is money.

2 Monitoring and rebalancing too infrequently.

Monitoring and rebalancing too infrequently may change the investor's risk and return trade-off profile to one that is not appropriate for his or her objectives and constraints. The less an investor or portfolio manager monitors and rebalances the greater the opportunity for asset classes to move undetected outside of allocation ranges. As a result, their risk and return trade-off profile will change, thus exposing the investor to either greater risk, or the potential for lower returns.

3 Overestimating or underestimating the impact of rebalancing costs.

By miscalculating the impact of rebalancing costs, an investor will either stop an otherwise prudent rebalancing action or prompt a rebalancing action that should not be made. Naturally, both outcomes are detriments to the risk and return trade-off profile of the portfolio.

4 Executing rebalancing incorrectly.

The sole focus of rebalancing is to keep a portfolio's risk and return trade-off profile in an acceptable range. Selling too much or too little of an overextended asset class or reallocating in the wrong proportion to underextended asset classes could place the portfolio on shaky ground going forward and expose it to additional rebalancing that, under normal circumstances, is not necessary.

Part 3

Additional Considerations

Chapter 9

From a Global Perspective

♦ ♦ ♦

Importance of Global Asset Allocation

Global financial markets have experienced dynamic changes over the last couple of decades. U.S. equities now account for less than half of the total global equity market capitalization. This figure is down from more than two-thirds just a couple decades ago. As a result, investors who incorporate international assets into their portfolios will find greater opportunities to protect and grow their investments. More specifically, they will improve the risk and return trade-off profile inherent in their portfolio by adding international assets to their asset mix. Consider for example two football teams, one with 45 players and one with 100 players. Since only 11 players are on the field at any one particular time, the chances of the team with 100 players to find better players is higher than the team with 45 players. Of course this is not the case in all situations, but it is for the vast majority of situations. It is simply the law of numbers. By the way, the numbers 45 and 100 were not selected at random. 45 is the approximate percentage of the global equity market the U.S. market represented in the mid 1990's, while the 100 simply represents the entire global equity market (100%).

Historically, most individual investors did not pay attention to investing globally for three principle reasons:

- Investors did not realize the benefits
- Transaction costs were substantial
- Information for making investment decisions was unreliable, or worse yet, absent.

Over the years, both transactions costs and availability of information have become more favorable and many investors have realized the benefits of adding international investments to their portfolios. According to the IMF, U.S. households have increased their percentage of foreign assets from 1.8% in the period from 1986 - 1990 to 6.6% in the period 1996 - 1999 (*World Economic Outlook*, October 2001, p. 75)

Adding international assets to an investment portfolio does not come without risk. There are new and different risks confronting the global investor. In addition, some risks that a U.S. investor faces are significantly magnified in foreign markets. For example, market liquidity is not as robust in most foreign countries as it is in the United States. Even with that being said, adding international assets to an investment portfolio still has more potential rewards than potential risks.

Why Invest Globally?

The ability of investors to reduce portfolio risk is limited in portfolios comprising purely U.S. assets. Investors are able to reduce total risk by minimizing company-specific risk. However, investors cannot reduce systematic risk, or risk attributed to the market and other uncontrollable external factors. That brings up a good question. What is the market? The market we have been talking about is the U.S. market. However, when investors add international assets to their portfolios, the market portfolio changes to encompass both the U.S. market and the foreign market from where the assets are added. Thus, reducing market risk is at the heart of global asset allocation.

FIGURE 10.1

Benefits of Global Investing

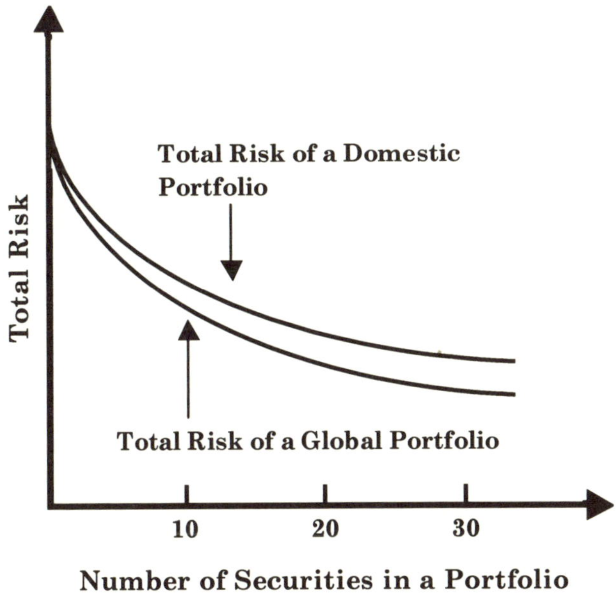

The reduction of total risk from global asset allocation is driven by the less than perfect correlations between U.S. assets and international assets. Going back to chapter three, we know that asset classes that are not perfectly positively correlated with each other will provide return enhancing and risk reducing.

Global correlations are different from country to country, some highly correlated to the U.S. and some not. Higher developed countries tend to have higher correlations with that of the U.S. and other developed countries due in large part to the significant degree of economic interaction. The more interaction among countries the more influence each country has on the economic conditions of the other. Conversely, the less interaction countries have with another, the more insulated they are from each other's economic influences, both positive and negative.

FIGURE 10.2

Correlations of Select Countries to U.S. Equity Returns

Country	Last 5 Years	Last 10 Years
Canada	0.78	0.78
Mexico	0.64	0.56
Australia	0.66	0.61
Hong Kong	0.65	0.59
Japan	0.45	0.44
New Zeeland	0.52	0.50
Singapore	0.63	0.55
France	0.74	0.70
Germany	0.76	0.73
Italy	0.59	0.51
Switzerland	0.66	0.67
Britain	0.83	0.78

Source: Frush Financial Group. Based on returns to July 2003.

Intuitively, one can see how the greatest benefits from adding international assets to a portfolio come from those countries that have the lowest correlations to the United States. However, the governments of many less-developed countries often place harsh regulations and severe restrictions on the investment and withdrawal of funds from their country. Higher potential returns come with higher potential risks.

Methods to Invest Globally

There are a number of methods you can use to add international assets to your portfolio. Some are quite effective while a couple offer only minor benefits.

Direct investments

Direct investments allow you to purchase assets via a foreign exchange, such as the London Stock Exchange or the Tokyo Stock Exchange. Unfortunately, there are a number of disadvantages to this method. First, it is significantly more difficult to obtain information on industries and companies in many foreign countries. Second, you generally face new and problematic investment regulations and restrictions unique to each country. Third, transaction costs (commissions and bid-ask spreads) associated with trading on foreign exchanges are usually higher, thus eroding the net return of an investment. Fourth, evaluating foreign assets for investment is challenging using U.S. analytical techniques. For example, different countries have different rules for what constitutes net income. Some countries allow certain accounting practices while others do not. As a result, earnings per share data from country to country are often not comparable. Thus, using the same analytical techniques is not always appropriate. Lastly, simply exchanging currency can often times be quite challenging.

Foreign assets listed on a U.S. exchange

This method can be summarized as, "Invest globally by investing locally". Instead of purchasing foreign assets via a foreign exchange, you purchase foreign assets directly on the New York

Stock Exchange (NYSE) or the American Stock Exchange (Amex). Shares of foreign companies such as Sony and Daimler-Chrysler are listed and traded on U.S. exchanges as well as on their home exchange.

Purchasing foreign investments on a U.S. exchange has some advantages over purchasing them on a foreign exchange. The advantages to this method are that you do not have to deal with currency exchange and that investment information is readily available. To be listed on the NYSE, the U.S. Securities and Exchange Commission requires foreign companies to conform to U.S. Generally Accepted Accounting Principals, or what is commonly referred to as GAAP. As a result, you are able to make much better evaluations and investment decisions. The major downside to this method is that most foreign companies do not list on a U.S. exchange, giving you a narrow list of investment options.

International mutual funds

International mutual funds are essentially the same as U.S. mutual funds in that they each comprise a pool of investments and are managed by a professional portfolio manager. The simple difference is that international mutual funds comprise international assets rather than U.S. assets. The concept of the international mutual fund has been around for quite some time. As a matter of fact, one of the very first hybrid international mutual funds was established back in the late 1700s in Holland. The fund was comprised of Russian and Mecklenburg government bonds, Bank of Vienna fixed-income securities, loans from the Spanish canal, English colonial securities, loans from South American plantations, and debt instruments from assorted Danish-American endeavors.

The advantage of international mutual funds is their specialized professional management. In addition, as with most mutual funds, international mutual funds offer immediate diversification and substantial liquidity to investors. International mutual funds allow you to build a portfolio with a relatively small investment. Finally, international mutual funds are denominated in U.S. dollars, thus eliminating the need and hassle of exchanging currency.

There are two primary disadvantages of international mutual funds. First, most target certain geographic regions of the globe. Consequently, the risk and return trade-off benefits received by you may be constrained. Investing in a group of international mutual funds where each targets different regions of the globe can help overcome this problem. Second, and most important, international mutual funds often have very high expenses and management fees, sometimes approaching two percent annually. This of course is in direct response to the specialized research and operating expenditures that are required to operate the fund.

International closed-end funds

Closed-end funds are similar to mutual funds in that they represent a pool of investments managed by a professional portfolio manager. In contrast, international closed-end funds are listed on U.S. exchanges and have a fixed number of shares outstanding. This particular characteristic is an advantage of international closed-end funds. As a result, portfolio managers do not need to keep cash on hand to meet shareholder withdrawals, which allows the fund to be fully invested at all time. In addition, during periods of market weakness, portfolio managers are not forced to sell investments to meet shareholder withdrawals. Eliminating the need to invest new money or to liquidate existing investments to meet shareholder withdrawals is advantageous, especially with international closed-end funds that target less-liquid and less developed countries.

Prices for international closed-end funds are determined entirely by market demand. As a result, international closed-end funds can trade at either a discount or a premium to the market value of their holdings (often referred to as net asset value or NAV). Buying an international closed-end fund then becomes more complex and requires greater analysis. However, investors can use the premium or discount to their advantage. For example, let's say there is a market crash in German equities. International closed-end funds targeting this region will see their net asset values decline proportionately to the loss in German equities. Now say equities in this region begin to rally, but investors remain cautious leading to lower demand for these closed-end funds than for the equities these funds hold. Over time, investors' interests increase and they begin to make purchases, resulting in shrinking discounts. Those investors who took advantage of the rally in German equities by purchasing a closed-end fund will have experienced a double benefit of rising NAVs and shrinking discounts. Today, many international closed-end funds trade with large discounts, sometimes as high as twenty percent. In addition, it is not surprising to see premiums and discounts last for a number of years.

Now that we have discussed the advantages of international closed-end funds, let's shift gears and quickly discuss the principle disadvantage. Most international closed-end funds are highly targeted investments, usually focusing on only one particular country or region. As a result, international closed-end funds do not provide a good method to add international assets to your investment portfolio. You would need to add a significant number of international closed-end funds representing different countries in order to achieve proper global asset allocation.

Stocks of global corporations

This method simply involves purchasing securities of U.S. global corporations without directly purchasing foreign securities. Since U.S. global corporations have operations across the globe, they will be impacted by each country they operate in. For example, if a corporation has a factory in country A and riots in that country cause a shutdown in operations, then the corporation will be impacted by a loss of revenue. This in turn will decrease corporate earnings to some degree. In theory this method appears sound. However, studies have shown that the stocks of U.S. global corporations trade very similarly to U.S. non-global corporations. Consequently, this method provides little in the way of benefits from global asset allocation.

American depository receipts

American Depository Receipts (ADRs) are stocks issued in the United States by large U.S. money center banks. Each ADR represents an ownership interest in a fixed number of shares of a foreign company. The major advantage of ADRs is that they trade either on a U.S. exchange or over-the-counter depending on whether or not the foreign company is registered with the SEC. As a result, ADRs are denominated in U.S. dollars thus eliminating the need to exchange currency. They can be bought and sold like U.S. stocks and their dividends are paid in U.S. dollars.

Being listed on a U.S. exchange allows an investor to trade the security and have the transaction completed much quicker. Unlike direct purchases on foreign exchanges, ADRs settle just as quickly and easily as U.S. stocks do. Thus, investors encounter less operational problems than do investors who purchase foreign securities directly.

Today there are more than 1,500 ADRs available for investment in the United States. Although ADRs have been in use since the 1920s, they have become increasingly more popular in recent years. The popularity of ADRs is primarily due to the greater interest and participation from foreign companies who view ADRs as a way raise needed capital, increase and diversify their base of shareholders, and create and enhance support for their goods and services in the U.S. marketplace.

Although ADRs are traded in U.S. dollars, their prices are indirectly influenced by currency exchange fluctuations. In general, the stronger the performance of the U.S. dollar versus a foreign currency, the worse your net investment return. In contrast, the weaker the performance of the U.S. dollar versus a foreign currency, the better your net investment return. Moreover, it is extremely difficult to forecast future exchange rates, thus leaving investors at the mercy of macroeconomic factors.

A disadvantage of ADRs is that some foreign corporations do not adhere to U.S. GAAP. Again, this problem creates more challenging evaluations and investment decision-making. Another disadvantage is that not all foreign corporations have underlying ADRs. Therefore, investors have fewer investment alternatives with this method.

Given the current trend toward increased globalization, the future for ADRs is murky at best. Why? The reason is because other methods of investing internationally will probably become more preferred. For example, the number of foreign stocks listed on U.S. exchanges will undoubtedly increase over time. Since money center banks will be out of the picture, transaction costs will decline. In addition, the quantity and quality of information on foreign companies will increase allowing for more informed evaluations and better investment decisions.

International index investments

International index investments may provide the best method for you to achieve global asset allocation. International index investments provide broad market exposure and high degrees of diversification at very low costs. International index investments trade on U.S. exchanges in about the same way as do shares of U.S. publicly traded companies. However, international index investments are not shares of a company. Rather, they are shares of a portfolio designed to closely track the performance of any number of market indices. Each international index investment closely tracks a specific market, offering an effective method to obtain cost-effective exposure to the markets and sectors desired.

Risks Associated With Global Investing

In aggregate, international investments generally offer higher return potential than U.S. investments. However, you should keep in mind that investing internationally typically involves increased risk. Nonetheless, international investments are still ideal since they are not perfectly positively correlated with U.S. investments and thus provide return enhancing and risk reducing benefits to your portfolio. International investments tend to be more risky than U.S. investments for the following reasons:

Currency fluctuation

Exchange rates between the U.S. dollar and foreign currencies are constantly changing due to supply and demand for each currency. As a result, currency exchange rates can substantially increase or decrease the net return (expressed in U.S. dollars) of your investment made abroad even if the market value of your investment did not change during the holding period.

Example: A U.S. real estate investment group purchases a commercial property in Canada for $500,000 Canadian dollars. If one year later the value of the property remains at $500,000 Canadian dollars and the Canadian dollar has declined in value versus the U.S. dollar, then the U.S. real estate investment group will experience a negative holding period return. Why? This reason is because if the U.S. real estate investment group were to sell the property, it would take more depreciated Canadian dollars to buy appreciated U.S. dollars.

Political

Political risk refers to the uncertainty that political decisions, policies, events and conditions in a foreign country will adversely impact the values of investments made in that particular country. Political risk takes many forms such as, trade agreements, severe tariffs, interference with operations, confiscation of property, economic instability, repatriation of profits, restrictions, war, revolution, terrorism and sabotage, kidnap & ransom, extortion, and lack of or reliability of financial information.

Lack of liquidity

You may find it challenging to trade securities in less-developed countries due to their smaller market size and resulting lower inherent supply and demand. In fact, at times there may be little to no demand for an investment that you need to sell. As a result, you may be forced to liquidate your investment at a much lower price than expected, even if detrimental to your net investment return.

Merging of asset correlations among countries

Over time, as global economies progressively become more integrated, so to do correlations among countries. This development is slow, but steady. Today, nearly 50% of the global market capitalization and 40% of global sales are attributed to multinational corporations. This trend will only become more pronounced as global corporations increase their global operations either through organic growth or through the acquisition of foreign companies. As a result of the rising correlations, the risk and return trade-off benefits from global asset allocation will lessen. However, as we have discussed previously, as long as correlations are not perfect, there is opportunity for you to enhance your returns while reducing your risk.

How Much Should You Allocate to International Assets?

There is a significant debate as to how much you should allocate to international assets. The best answer is to base the allocation on your risk tolerance. For those investors who aspire for a higher return and are willing and able to assume a higher risk, they can allocate a substantial portion of their portfolio to international assets, possibly close to 50%. Conversely, for those investors who have lower risk tolerances and lower return aspirations, they can allocate a much smaller portion, if any, of their portfolio to international assets, possibly anywhere from 5 – 15%.

Given the risks of investing globally, adding international assets to an investment portfolio requires greater analysis and evaluation. Although you may have the ability to perform these tasks, you may still want to seek professional counsel.

Chapter 10

The 10 Cornerstone Principles of Asset Allocation

♦ ♦ ♦

Of the three investment strategies (i.e. asset allocation, security selection, market timing) asset allocation has been shown to be the primary determinant of investment performance. As a matter of fact, some studies show that asset allocation determines approximately ten times more of a portfolio's performance than both security selection and market timing combined!

Asset allocation is underscored by a number of important principles, each of which has been discussed at length throughout this book. To better help you to understand and conceptualize asset allocation, I have assembled the most important of these principles, or those that I refer to as the cornerstone principles. The process of building your optimal investment portfolio requires you or your portfolio manager to incorporate each of the following cornerstone principles into the designing, constructing, monitoring and rebalancing phases of portfolio management.

The following is the list of the ten cornerstone principles of asset allocation:

1 Specific financial goals

Knowing why you are investing is the vital first step with asset allocation. Once you know why, only then can you establish your return aspiration.

During the process of establishing your specific financial goals, it is highly important they be prioritized and quantified. Simply saying you need enough money to fund a college education or support yourself and your spouse in retirement is much too ambiguous and not especially intelligent. Identifying that you need $25,000 per year for four years in today's dollars or $75,000 per year in retirement expressed in today's dollars is more appropriate.

Lastly, when identifying your specific financial goals, you need to make sure they are achievable and measurable. For example, determining you need a 25% annual return for twenty years to accumulate $2,000,000 for retirement is measurable, but far from achievable.

2 Willingness to tolerate risk

Risk tolerance is perhaps the most important cornerstone principle of asset allocation. Your optimal portfolio is predominantly designed based on your willingness and ability to tolerant risk.

Once your risk tolerance is determined, your optimal asset mix can then be established in order to maximize your portfolio's return potential. The best method to identify your risk tolerance is to complete a risk-based questionnaire available through most investment advisors or mutual fund companies. Appendix A of this book provides such a questionnaire.

Personal preferences toward risk assumption play a vital role in determining your willingness to tolerate risk. For example, you could take two different investors with the same level of wealth and the same specific financial goals and find that each has a different preference for assuming risk. Occupation, sex, age and education have been shown to influence an investor's willingness to assume risk. This is the key reason why the definition of Optimal Investing includes the risk an investor is *willing* and *able* to assume.

3 Ability to tolerate risk

Your ability to tolerate risk is highly contingent on your time horizon and level of wealth. All else being equal, the greater your time horizon and your level of wealth the more risk tolerant you can be. Why? Intuitively one can see how those with longer time horizons and those with greater levels of wealth have more room for error in achieving their specific financial goals. Of course this is not always the case, but as a general rule it usually holds true. For instance, if you were to win the lottery, your ability to tolerate risk would increase dramatically. Wouldn't you care less about losing $10,000 if you just won $50,000,000?

In practice, there are four stages of wealth, or what are referred to as lifecycle phases. These include the accumulation phase, consolidation phase, spending phase, and gifting phase. Most investors begin their lives in the accumulation phase and by the time they are well into their golden years they are in the gifting phase. Each of these phases provides a hint as to the length of time horizon and level of wealth an investor possesses and therefore what his or her ability to tolerate risk might be.

4 Expected total rate of return

Total rate of return is the sum of an investment's appreciation plus income (interest and dividends) received over the holding period all divided by the initial dollar investment. Expected total return is simply you or your portfolio manager's forecast of total return for each asset class and asset subclass during the future holding period. Why is expected total return a cornerstone principle? The reason is because the design of the optimal portfolio relies on this forecast.

Once your risk tolerance has been identified, you must design your portfolio to maximize expected total rate of return for the given level of risk you are willing and able to assume. This task cannot be accomplished without the knowledge of returns. This is the essence of the risk and return trade-off profile. Without a clear understanding of expected total rates of return for each asset class, there is little hope of maximizing your portfolio's performance and building your optimal portfolio.

5 Risk and return trade-off profile

The trade-off between risk and return is central to the application of asset allocation theory to an investment portfolio. These two concepts are unequivocally linked. One simply cannot earn an excessive return while assuming a corresponding low risk. Any promise to the contrary by an investment professional is a sure sign of investment fraud.

In basic asset allocation theory, the higher your risk tolerance the higher the potential return you should earn. You should not assume higher risk for the same potential return as a less risky asset may offer. The message here is that you need to build a portfolio where the expected rates of return are maximized for the given level of risk you are willing and able to assume.

6 Optimal asset mix

Asset class mix refers to both the asset classes and asset subclasses you have allocated investments to and their respective weightings within your optimal portfolio. It is essential to allocate your portfolio's investments in a deliberate way to create your desired risk and return trade-off profile. Thus, allocating your investments to those asset classes and asset subclasses to create your desired risk and return trade-off profile defines your optimal asset mix. Misallocating your investments will create a situation where your portfolio either assumes more risk than appropriate or where the portfolio does not assume enough risk thereby placing the portfolio in a position where the chances of achieving your specific financial goals are in jeopardy.

Unfortunately, the work does not stop once your portfolio is designed with the optimal asset mix. Rebalancing is key to keeping your asset mix in balance with your optimal asset mix. Rebalancing is cornerstone principle #10.

7 Correlation

The term correlation refers to how closely two asset class prices move in relation to one another. Although not always the case, most securities within an asset class or asset subclass tend to move together over time. Of course there are always exceptions.

Your goal is to allocate investments to asset classes and asset subclasses that do not move in perfect lock-step form with each other. The greater the difference, or lower correlation, two asset classes move together, the more attractive they are for possible investment purposes. Since some asset classes experience strength at one time while others experience strength at other times, it is essential to be invested in multiple asset classes at all times. Investing in multiple asset classes allows you to avoid serious market and portfolio weakness. By investing in multiple asset classes with low correlations, you enhance your expected return while at the same time reduce the risk you have assumed.

8 Time horizon

Time horizon plays a significant role in determining expectations for asset class total returns, risk and correlations. As mentioned in other cornerstone principles, making accurate forecasts are essential to building your optimal portfolio.

The primary use of time horizon is to help determine the portfolio balance between equity assets and assets that emphasize current income, namely fixed-income and cash & equivalents. All else being equal, the longer your time horizon the more equity investments and less current income producing investments you should incorporate. Conversely, the shorter your time horizon the more current income producing investments and less equity investments you should incorporate.

The most common risk you need to address over the long-term is purchasing power risk, or the loss of an asset's real value due to inflation. Equity investments provide the best defense against inflation. As a result, the longer your time horizon, the more you should allocate to equity assets. In the short-term, the most common risk is volatility. Fixed-income investments pro-vide the best defense against this type of risk and should be emphasized in your portfolio as a result.

One last thought about time horizon. Many investors mistakenly assume their time horizon lasts until they retire. This could not be further from the truth. Your time horizon is the period from the present to the point in the future where you no longer need the assets in your portfolio.

9 Diversification

Diversification is critical to minimize the overall risk within your portfolio. Contrary to misconception, diversification is not the same as asset allocation and the two concepts should not be confused.

The process of diversifying your portfolio should be addressed after completing the process of allocating your wealth among asset classes and asset subclasses. Diversification is the process of investing in a significant number of securities within each asset class in order to reduce, if not eliminate altogether, the risk associated with each individual security, namely company-specific risk. By investing in a significant number of securities, the impact of a poor management decision, for example, from one of the companies you invested in will be minimized. To achieve the greatest benefits, you should diversify all of your holdings (equities, fixed-income, real estate, commodities, etc.) and not just select asset classes or asset subclasses. However, due to the significant amount of inherent company-specific risk, your equity investments will experience the greatest benefit from diversification.

It is important to understand that the process of diversification entails investing in securities with similar risk and return trade-off profiles. By doing so, the risk and return trade-off profile desired for your overall portfolio will remain constant.

10 Rebalancing

Over time, the asset mix within your portfolio changes due to price fluctuations. As a result, your portfolio's risk and return trade-off profile will change with changes to your asset mix. Rebalancing is the process of selling and buying investments in order to return your current asset class weightings to your optimal asset mix. Rebalancing involves selling those asset classes that have become overweighed and buying those asset classes that have become underweighted.

Rebalancing is key to achieving your specific financial goals. Rebalancing is more important than your optimal asset mix.

Chapter 11

Model Investment Portfolios

♦ ♦ ♦

People in the Accumulation Lifecycle Phase

Profile: Typically people in their early careers with a long-term time horizon. Their net worth, and sometimes their income, is small relative to their debt.

Common Goals:

- Establish a career
- Upgrade auto
- Start a family
- Begin saving for retirement
- Buy or upgrade a home

- Pay down student loans
- Increase liquidity
- Begin saving for children's education

Common Objectives:

Return Aspiration:
With a long-term time horizon, people in the accumulation lifecycle phase should seek total returns by focusing their portfolios on capital gain, growth-oriented assets. At the same time, people in this phase need to be cognizant of current income to help with immediate spending goals.

Risk Tolerance:
Due to their long-term time horizon, people in this phase have the ability to tolerate a high level of risk.

Common Constraints:

Time Horizon:
The time horizon for people in the accumulation lifecycle phase is very long, sometimes as long as 70+ years.

Liquidity Needs:
People in this phase have a moderate to high need for liquidity given their immediate spending needs.

Tax Considerations:
Estate, trust and other tax considerations are low for people in this phase. The most important taxes to consider are capital gains and income. Given their long-term time horizon and from a tax perspective, growth-oriented assets are preferable over income-oriented assets. However, the need for income-oriented assets must be balanced with growth-oriented assets to cover current spending needs.

FEW MODERATE NUMEROUS

Legal & Regulatory Considerations:
Most people in this phase will have very few legal and regulatory issues to contend with. The most common issues arising will be related to contributions and withdrawals from retirement accounts, namely IRAs and 401ks. Wills and related legal documents should be completed at this time.

FEW MODERATE NUMEROUS

Unique Circumstances & Preferences:
For people in this phase, unique circumstances and preferences could include, single-parent families, financially supporting an adult parent, or paying child support.

FEW MODERATE NUMEROUS

Target Optimal Asset Mix:

Asset Class	Allocation Range %
Cash & equivalents	5 – 10
Fixed-income	5 – 15
Equities	70 – 90
Alternatives	0 – 5

Summary:

It is rather cut and dry with people in the accumulation lifecycle phase. Their focus should be targeted toward growth-oriented assets and have investment plans that emphasize long-term time horizons. Vitally important is the creation of a financial plan and the Investment Policy Statement.

PEOPLE IN THE CONSOLIDATION LIFECYCLE PHASE

Profile: Typically people in their middle to late working years when their time horizon is still relatively long. As they progress through this phase, their income begins to exceed their expenses.

Common Goals:

- Progress in career
- Upgrade auto
- Start or expand family
- Grow retirement savings
- Upgrade home
- Buy second home
- Take more vacations
- Open a business

Common Objectives:

Return Aspiration:
With a long-term time horizon, people in the consolidation lifecycle phase should seek total returns by focusing their portfolios on capital gain, growth-oriented assets. In addition, more emphasis should be placed on reallocating assets to less risky investments as they progress through this lifecycle phase.

▼

LOW **MODERATE** **HIGH**

Risk Tolerance:
Due to their long-term time horizon, people in this phase have the ability to tolerate an above average level of risk.

LOW MODERATE ▼ HIGH

Common Constraints:

Time Horizon:
The time horizon for people in the consolidation lifecycle phase is long, anywhere from 20 to 40+ years.

SHORT MODERATE ▼ LONG

Liquidity Needs:
People in this phase have a low need for liquidity since their incomes tend to exceed their expenses.

LOW ▼ MODERATE HIGH

Tax Considerations:
Most tax considerations remain low, but some new considerations begin appearing, such as trust taxes. As with the accumulation lifecycle phase, given their long-term time horizon and from a tax perspective, growth-oriented assets are preferable over income-oriented assets.

FEW ▼ MODERATE NUMEROUS

Legal & Regulatory Considerations:
As people begin to approach retirement, their legal and regulatory issues occur more frequently. People in this phase will need to update their Wills and emphasize estate planning. In

addition, penalty free distributions from retirement plans cannot be made until age 59½.

▼

FEW	MODERATE	NUMEROUS

Unique Circumstances & Preferences:
Such unique circumstances and preferences could include forced early retirement, single-parent families, financially supporting an adult parent or disabled child or bankruptcy from a failed business.

▼

FEW	MODERATE	NUMEROUS

Target Optimal Asset Mix:

Asset Class	Allocation Range %
Cash & equivalents	5 – 10
Fixed-income	20 – 35
Equities	45 – 75
Alternatives	0 – 10

Summary:

People in the consolidation lifecycle phase will need to focus on growing and protecting their retirement portfolios. Maximizing contributions to retirement and non-retirement portfolios is vital. People in this phase should begin reallocating a small portion of their portfolios out of equities and primarily into fixed-income as they age. As a result, the risk of the portfolio will decrease thus helping to protect the portfolio from significant market weakness. Also of critical importance is the need to address estate planning.

People in the Spending Lifecycle Phase

Profile: Typically people in their late careers to early retirement with time horizons ranging anywhere from 7 to 20+ years. As a result, most people in this lifecycle phase have moderate to long-term time horizons. For many, their expenses exceed their income in retirement, which is supplemented by investment and retirement income.

Common Goals:

- Retire
- Take more vacations
- Spend time with children and grandchildren
- Protect retirement savings
- Move to a warmer climate
- Downsize house and other assets
- Donate time and wealth to philanthropic organizations

Common Objectives:

Return Aspiration:
With moderate to long-term time horizons, people in the spending lifecycle phase should seek total returns by balancing their portfolios between growth-oriented and income-oriented assets. In addition, more emphasis should be placed on reallocating assets to more conservative assets, such as cash & equivalents, as they progress through this lifecycle phase.

▼

LOW	MODERATE	HIGH

Risk Tolerance:
Given a more modest time horizon, people in the spending lifecycle phase have lower tolerances for risk than those of the aforementioned lifecycle phases. Their risk tolerance is consid-

ered low to moderate. Higher wealth levels will enhance one's tolerance for risk.

▼

LOW MODERATE HIGH

Common Constraints:

Time Horizon:
The time horizon for people in this lifecycle phase is moderate to long, anywhere from 7 to 20+ years.

▼

SHORT MODERATE LONG

Liquidity Needs:
People in the spending lifecycle phase have a moderate need for liquidity since their spending exceeds their income. Those in this phase who have not yet retired have low needs for liquidity.

▼

LOW MODERATE HIGH

Tax Considerations:
The number and complexity of tax considerations begins to increase in this phase. Although people in this phase need to balance taxes on capital gains and income (dividends and interest), they also need to focus on estate tax planning, tax-exempt investments and trust tax considerations.

▼

FEW MODERATE NUMEROUS

Legal & Regulatory Considerations:
The most common legal and regulatory issues experienced in this phase are those regarding distributions from retirement plans and those related to distributions from estates.

▼

FEW **MODERATE** **NUMEROUS**

Unique Circumstances & Preferences:
Their unique circumstances and preferences could include sickness, disability or sale of a family business.

▼

FEW **MODERATE** **NUMEROUS**

Target Optimal Asset Mix:

Asset Class	Allocation Range %
Cash & equivalents	15 – 25
Fixed-income	35 – 50
Equities	20 – 50
Alternatives	0 – 5

Summary:

Since people in this phase are typically spending more than their income, liquidity becomes a pressing need. In addition, a reallocation from equities to fixed-income assets is prudent given the low to moderate tolerance for risk. Upon retirement, stronger emphasis should be placed on income-oriented assets to help offset the loss of employment income in order to support one's lifestyle in retirement. Estate planning documents should be evaluated and updated to address current circumstances.

PEOPLE IN THE GIFTING LIFECYCLE PHASE

Profile: Typically people well into their retirement years when their time horizon is becoming shorter. In this phase, an individual owns more assets than he or she will ever need.

Common Goals:

- Distribute wealth to family and philanthropic organizations
- Spend time with family
- Sustain good health
- Take more vacations
- Protect retirement savings
- Move to a warmer climate
- Become a mentor to younger people

Common Objectives:

Return Aspiration:
With a short to moderate time horizon, people in the gifting lifecycle phase should seek total returns by focusing their portfolios principally on fixed-income assets, with some growth-oriented equity assets included.

Risk Tolerance:
Given their shorter time horizon, people in the gifting lifecycle phase have a low to moderate tolerance for risk. People in this lifecycle phase with substantial wealth will naturally have a higher tolerance for risk, possibly moderate to high.

Common Constraints:

Time Horizon:
At 70+ in age, the time horizon for people in this lifecycle phase is short to moderate.

Liquidity Needs:
People in the gifting lifecycle phase have an above average need for liquidity since their primary common goal is to have funds available to distribute to family members and charitable organizations.

Tax Considerations:
Tax management is again at the forefront for people in this phase. Estate tax considerations become the most prevalent tax consideration in this lifecycle phase.

Legal & Regulatory Considerations:
As with people in the spending lifecycle phase, those in the gifting phase confront issues related to distributions (including mandatory distributions from retirement plans) and those related to distributions from estates.

Unique Circumstances & Preferences:
Unique circumstances and preferences could include sickness or disability, or even the disposal of a large estate.

▼

FEW	MODERATE	NUMEROUS

Target Optimal Asset Mix:

Asset Class	Allocation Range %
Cash & equivalents	20 – 30
Fixed-income	30 – 45
Equities	20 – 50
Alternatives	0 – 5

Summary:

The main concern facing this group is liquidity to facilitate the distribution of their wealth. Given the need for more liquidity, a reallocation out of growth-oriented investments and to income-oriented investments is prudent. Before entering this lifecycle phase, estate planning should have been addressed and completed. Evaluations and revisions to estate planning documents and their Investment Policy Statement are appropriate each year or when their financial situation changes.

Chapter 12

15 Golden Rules for Building Your Optimal Portfolio

♦ ♦ ♦

An investment in knowledge always pays the best interest.

– Benjamin Franklin

Over the years I have had the distinct pleasure of working with many very successful individual and institutional investors. In addition, I have been fortunate to work with a number of very intelligent and influential analysts, portfolio managers and investment strategists. From my experience I have discovered some very important rules that enable investors to gain an edge over other investors. After reviewing and analyzing the rules exhibited by successful investors, I have compiled a list of the most important ones. These rules are the foundation for the successful optimal investor. Without further ado, 15 golden rules for building your optimal portfolio are:

1 Apply asset allocation theory to your portfolio and adhere to it.

Asset allocation has been shown to explain the vast majority of your investment performance. As a result, it is essential that you adopt a sound asset allocation plan and apply it to the management of your portfolio. In addition, make sure that you understand and implement the 10 cornerstone principles of asset allocation from chapter ten.

2 Identify your specific financial goals.

A majority of investors begin investing before truly identifying their specific financial goals. By identifying your specific financial goals, you can tailor the management of your portfolio, investments, focus, style and strategy to achieve these specific financial goals efficiently and successfully.

3 Establish realistic, achievable and measurable goals.

Identifying your specific financial goals is only half the battle. Making sure they are realistic, achievable and measurable given the level of risk you are willing and able to assume is another. Establishing goals that are not realistic, achievable or measurable will cause some investors to assume more risk than appropriate and others to underperform expectations.

Chance favors the prepared mind.

– Louis Pasteur

4 Identify your true risk tolerance.

The primary goal of asset allocation is to maximize your expected total rate of return for the level of risk you are willing and able to assume. Consequently, it is very important that you identify your true risk tolerance as everything else will fall into place. Your optimal asset mix is dependent on your desired risk and return trade-off profile. The message here is that attaining specific financial goals can only be tackled after identifying your true risk tolerance.

5 Understand the fundamental characteristics of each asset class.

It is not necessary for you to know highly detailed and complex information about each asset class and asset subclass. Rather, it is important that you have a strong command of the underlying advantages, disadvantages and reasons for investing in each asset class and asset subclass. Knowing that equity securities are your best defense against purchasing power risk and that fixed-income securities are your best defense against volatility risk is vital.

6 Select your optimal asset mix.

Achieving your specific financial goals is dependent on your portfolio's risk and return trade-off profile. Your optimal asset mix, or the asset classes and asset subclasses you invest in and in what proportion, is the driving force behind developing your desired risk and return trade-off profile. Remember that one of the most important tasks with selecting your optimal asset mix is to balance equities with both fixed-income and cash and equivalents. The longer your time horizon, the more emphasis you need to place on equities. Your optimal asset mix should emphasize fixed-income and cash & equivalents when your time horizon is short-term.

7 Focus on your portfolio rather than the individual investments comprising your portfolio.

One of the biggest mistakes investors can make is to focus on certain investments within their portfolio than focusing on their portfolio as a whole. It is important to realize that portfolios behave in a much different way than do the individual investments comprising a portfolio. Thus, a portfolio comprising only fixed-income investments will actually make your portfolio more risky, with a lower expected return, than a portfolio comprising both fixed-income and equity investments. Investors who desire a more conservative portfolio should therefore own some less risky investments and some more risky investments.

8 Diversify the securities within each asset class.

One of the best methods of reducing total risk is to diversify within each asset class. Diversification involves purchasing numerous securities with the same risk and return trade-off profile. Doing so will reduce the negative impact of any one security within the portfolio. On the whole, diversification within equity securities is most beneficial since equity securities posses the greatest amount of company-specific risk. Index investments provide the best way for you to diversify your portfolio as they essentially contain all of the securities within that market.

9 Do not attempt to time the market.

Study after study has shown that market timing determines only a small portion of your total investment performance over time. As a result, focusing on this strategy is generally a waste of time and resources. Rather than attempting to time the market, reallocate your time and resources to monitoring and rebalancing your portfolio.

10 Identify and incorporate tax implications into your decision process.

Capital gains taxes can have a severe impact on the performance of your portfolio. As a result, your decision to sell a security or securities should be made with the knowledge and understanding of how taxes will impact your portfolio's performance. However, it is important to remember that your decision should emphasize appropriateness and suitability of the investment first. The impact of taxes always takes a back seat to appropriateness and suitability. Beware of taxes, but never hold a security that is not suitable.

11 Understand that recent returns are no indication of future returns.

Many investors have a misconception that the recent past is an indicator of the future. As a result, they over allocate to those asset classes that have been generating strong returns over the most recent time period. These investors mistakenly think the momentum will continue into the foreseeable future. Unfortunately this is a mistake since asset classes frequently rotate price leadership.

> *Pension fund managers continue to make decisions with their eyes firmly fixed in the rear-view mirror.*
>
> – Warren Buffett

12 Invest for the long-term.

It is difficult, if not impossible, to predict future short-term asset class returns. However, this task becomes significantly less difficult as the holding period increases. Having confidence in future returns allows for the selection of your optimal asset mix. Depending on an investor's goals, investing for the short-term can be a form of market timing.

13 Understand that investing is a process.

It is very important to understand that investing is a process and not a one-time event. Investing involves establishing objecttives and constraints, as well as designing, constructing, monitoring and rebalancing your optimal portfolio. Each phase of the process depends on the other and should be executed with precision. No investor will ever be successful by simply approaching investing as a one-time event, such as constructing an investment portfolio and omitting the monitoring and rebalancing phases.

14 Draft an Investment Policy Statement (IPS).

An IPS is critical to the long-term achievement of your specific financial goals. An Investment Policy Statement should encompass and accommodate all of the above golden rules. For example, a sound IPS assists you to more fully identify what your specific financial goals are (golden rule #2) and ensure they are realistic, achievable and measurable (golden rule #3). In addition, a sound IPS defines your true risk tolerance (golden rule #4) and outlines your optimal asset mix (golden rule #6).

15 Remain committed to your plan.

In the short-term, it is easy to follow through and remain committed to your plan. Following through on your plan over the long-term is another story and is much easier said than done. However, it is vital that investors do just that. A sound plan is only as good as how well it is executed over your entire investment time horizon.

Diamonds are only lumps of coal that stuck to their jobs.
– B.C. Forbes

Chapter 13

Obtaining Professional Counsel

♦ ♦ ♦

Importance of Professional Counsel

This book is intended to give you all of the tools and resources required to easily and successfully design, construct, monitor, and rebalance your optimal portfolio. However, this book is not intended to be a complete substitute for experienced professional assistance and counsel in every situation. In an endeavor as critical as managing your optimal portfolio, it is not prudent to handle every situation without the help of a competent professional advisor. Furthermore many individual investors simply do not have the time, patience, and persistence to deal effectively with their investments over the long-term. Many investors do have the motivation to put in the required time to fully address their investments at the outset, but become less motivated as time goes by. In addition, there are some very common mistakes that individual investors make that a professional will help to overcome. These mistakes include:

- Focusing more time and effort on security selection and market timing than on the most important determinant, asset allocation.
- Making ad hoc fear-based revisions at the first sign of market weakness.
- Having unrealistic goals and return expectations.
- Omitting the process of drafting an Investment Policy Statement.
- Emphasizing individual securities rather than emphasizing the overall portfolio.
- Failing to reevaluate their financial situation at least annually and then revising their Investment Policy Statement.
- Getting caught up in the hype of the market and losing investment focus.

Evaluating Professional Counsel

Obtaining professional counsel is a significant step unto itself and should not be approached lightly. As with investors and their objectives and constraints, professional advisors also differ in their philosophy, processes, services, education, experience, and their ability to add value. Professional advisors work in many fields and hold varied titles, such as investment advisor, financial planner, accountant, estate planner, insurance agent, and stockbroker. Over the last few years, most professional advisors have seen their roles expand and now the lines among them have become greatly blurred. Today it is now commonplace to meet an insurance agent who is also registered as an investment advisor or a stockbroker who engages in the practice of estate planning.

With so many potential professional investment advisors to select from, the process can seem daunting. Remember, not all professional advisors are equal! Some advisors may say the same things as others, but some are simply slick talking salespeople. The following are some important questions you should investigate regarding a potential advisor:

Question 1: *Is the advisor highly qualified?*

What education does the advisor have? Bachelors? Masters? You would be surprised at the number of advisors I have met who have either no bachelors degrees or degrees in a field not even related to finance and investing (dance – yes, I met one with this degree!). You should also make sure the advisor has professional designations, such as the CPA (Certified Public Accountant), CFP (Certified Financial Planner), CFA (Chartered Financial Analyst), or ChFC (Chartered Financial Consultant). Having a designation illustrates commitment and very specialized knowledge.

Question 2: *What is the advisor's investment philosophy?*

You should make sure that the advisor incorporates asset allocation into their investment philosophy and applies it to their portfolio management process. You would be floored at the number of advisors who wing it when designing portfolios because they either have no philosophy or fail to adopt one. Also, you should consider investigating whether or not the advisor adopts some sort of plan that includes the 15 golden rules for building your optimal portfolio.

Question 3: *What is the advisor's experience?*

You should find out how long the advisor has been in practice and how long they have been in their present role. A follow up question could address the advisor's specific work experience. Also, do not be fooled by the advisor's age. I have known many advisors who entered the business late in their careers and consequently had as much to offer as someone straight out of college.

Question 4: *What services does the advisor offer?*

It is important to first determine what services you are seeking: investment counseling, total financial planning, estate planning, and/or tax preparation. Once this question is answered, you should investigate whether or not the advisor offers these services. This is important because most professional advisors do not offer a complete array of services. It is common for advisors either to have relationships with outside advisors who can address the areas not serviced or, if their firm is large enough, to have someone else in their firm handle separate services.

Question 5: *What are the fees?*

Most advisors will be able to provide you with a written document outlining their fees. If the advisor cannot provide this, bypass this advisor.

Question 6: *How are fees paid?*

There are many ways an advisor can be compensated: commission, a percentage of your portfolio market value, hourly fees, fees for individual services performed, or any combination of them. There is not any true right or wrong fee structure. The best fee structure is what makes sense and is the best fit for you. Personally, I recommend investors seek advisors with asset-sized fees. Under this scenario, a typical investor will pay anywhere from ½% to 1½% of their portfolio market value in fees to the advisor. This structure is appealing because it motivates the advisor to grow your portfolio, thereby growing his or her fees at the same time. Essentially, one can say that an asset-sized fee structure aligns your interests with the interests of your advisor.

Question 7: *How ethical and trustworthy is the advisor?*

This question is obviously very subjective and not always easy to answer. Aside from your intuition, the options for addressing this are limited. A good way to approach this question is to investigate whether or not either a regulatory organization or a private association he or she might be a member of has publicly disciplined him or her. To check on an advisor's regulatory record, you should contact the NASD (National Association of Securities Dealers) or any association the advisor may be a member of, such as the Certified Financial Planning Board of Standards (www.CFP.net).

Question 8: *What is the long-term investment performance of the advisor?*

The vast majority of advisors can provide you with some sort of performance composite for you to review. When reviewing performance information be sure to learn which benchmark or benchmarks are employed (such as the S&P 500), how well the advisor performed against the benchmark or benchmarks, the consistency of performance over long periods of time, the volatility of performance (especially in relation to the benchmark or benchmarks), the growth of assets under management, and the statement of whether or not the performance conforms to AIMR (Association for Investment Management and Research) standards. If any of these items are not provided, ask the advisor to provide them. If the performance was not created according to AIMR standards, ask why. Performance is suspect when the advisor has not conformed to any standards, especially tough AIMR standards. AIMR is the organization that oversees the Chartered Financial Analyst (CFA) designation.

Question 9: *How does the advisor approach issues of tax management?*

You would be surprised with how some advisors approach the tax management issue. Some advisors underemphasize tax management while others overemphasize it. Specifically, ask about the general degree of turnover, how they incorporate tax management into the rebalancing phase, whether or not they can incorporate tax losses or gains generated outside of the portfolio and how they approach the issue of loss-harvesting and exchange strategies.

Question 10: *Is there a personality fit?*

The last question deals with whether or not you can work with the advisor. This question is more intuitive-oriented rather than objective-oriented. Usually after the first meeting you will know if there is a fit or not. Is the advisor more serious or humorous? Is the advisor intense or low-key? Is the advisor more professional or down-to-earth? Is he or she married, single or divorced? Does he or she play golf? Did a friend refer you? Are your interests similar? Etc, etc.

> *If you aren't fired with enthusiasm, you will be fired with enthusiasm.*
>
> – Vince Lombardi

In addition to the questions presented, another good way to evaluate an investment advisor is to review what is called Form ADV Part II. This form is required by the Securities and Exchange Commission (SEC) and the state of domicile of all advisors who hold themselves out as investment advisors. In addition, all investment advisors are required to provide this document to prospects before any services are provided. If you do not receive one, be sure to ask.

Making Sense of Advisors' Designations

The investment field has become an alphabet soup, so to speak, of professional designations. Most advisors obtain these designations for two reasons, to set themselves apart from the pack and to gain the education to move their business forward. When searching for professional help, you should place significant emphasis on advisors who have earned the right to use one or more of the following foremost designations. They are ranked in no particular order and no one or two designations suggests an advisor is more qualified than another advisor.

Registered Investment Advisor (RIA):

The term RIA technically describes an investment firm rather than a particular individual. These firms generally charge a percentage fee that is based on the market value of the assets in your portfolio. To be designated a Registered Investment Advisor, a firm must register with either the Securities and Exchange Commission or their state of domicile.

Certified Financial Planner (CFP):

The CFP designation is one of the most recognizable and most prestigious designations to obtain for the professional advisor. Professionals with the CFP designation are well grounded in all aspects of financial planning. Areas comprising the CFP include investment planning, estate planning, income tax planning, insurance and risk management, retirement planning and general financial planning. The CFP certificant, as they are called, must pass a number of exams, accumulate three years of related work experience and complete ongoing continuing education to quality for the designation.

Certified Fund Specialist (CFS):

The CFS designation provides a way for advisors to focus their business on mutual funds. Applicants must pass an exam on such topics as investment companies, performance measurement and asset allocation. Similar to the CFP, the CFS requires their designation holders to complete ongoing continuing education credits.

Certified Public Accountant (CPA):

The CPA designation is also one of the most recognizable designations and one of the hardest to obtain. In addition to earning accounting college credits, applicants are required to accumulate two years of work experience and pass a comprehensive exam. The focus of CPAs is geared toward tax preparation although more and more CPAs are entering the financial and investment planning fields.

Personal Financial Specialist (PFS):

CPAs who wish to concentrate specifically in financial planning have the opportunity to obtain the PFS designation. This designation is awarded only to CPAs in good standing with the AICPA. This designation covers topics such as estate planning, budgeting and saving, managing credit and retirement planning.

Chartered Financial Analyst (CFA):

Along with the CPA designation, the CFA may be perhaps the most difficult designation to earn. I can personally attest to its difficulty. The CFA applicant must pass three rigorous examinations and accumulate three years of professional work experience in the investment field. The CFA is a common designation for investment counselors, portfolio managers, mutual fund managers, and investment analysts.

Chartered Investment Counselor (CIC):

CFA designation holders who wish to demonstrate their knowledge and extensive work experience have the option of earning the CIC designation. CIC applicants must first obtain the CFA designation, be employed by a member firm of the ICAA (Investment Counsel Association of America), and must have accumulated at least five cumulative years of investment work experience.

Chartered Financial Consultant (ChFC):

The ChFC is very similar in focus to the CFP. The ChFC demonstrates broad knowledge of the financial planning field, such as estate planning, insurance and investment planning. Similar to CFPs, applicants must accumulate a specific amount of work experience before earning this designation.

Chartered Life Underwriter (CLU):

The CLU designation is targeted to insurance professionals. Contrary to its name, the CLU is not limited to only life insurance professionals. Many other professionals not employed in the life insurance field have earned the right to use it. Applicants for the CLU designation must complete a ten-course curriculum.

Chartered Mutual Fund Counselor (CMFC):

Similar to the CFS, the CMFC is a designation tailored to those who work with mutual funds. To obtain this designation, CMFC applicants must complete a self-study program and final examination on various mutual fund topics.

Chapter 14

Additional Resources

♦ ♦ ♦

Suggested Books

Getting Started in Asset Allocation
Eric Gelb & William Bresnan ISBN 0471326844

Global Asset Allocation
Techniques for Optimizing Portfolio Management
Jess Lederman & Robert Klein ISBN 0471593737

Global Asset Allocation
New Methods and Applications
Heinz Zimmermann, Peter Oertmann, & Wolfgang Drobetz ISBN 0471264261

Strategic Asset Allocation
Portfolio Choice for Long-term Investors
John Y. Campbell & Luis M. Viceira
ISBN 0198296940

Advanced Theory and Methodology of Tactical Asset Allocation
Wai Lee ISBN 1883249724

The Intelligent Asset Allocator
How to Build Your Portfolio to Maximize Returns and Minimize Risk
William Bernstein ISBN 0071362363

Asset Allocation
Balancing Financial Risk
Roger C. Gibson ISBN 0071357246

Efficient Asset Management
A Practical Guide to Stock Portfolio Optimization and Asset Allocation
Richard O. Michaud ISBN 0875847439

Common Sense on Mutual Funds
New Imperatives for the Intelligent Investor
John C. Bogle, Peter L. Bernstein ISBN 0471392286

A Random Walk Down Wall Street
The Time-Tested Strategy for Successful Investing
Burton G. Malkiel ISBN 0393057828

The Intelligent Investor
Benjamin Graham, Jason Zweig ISBN 0060555661

The Wall Street Journal Guide to Understanding Money & Investing
Kenneth M. Morris, Virginia B. Morris, Alan M. Siegel
ISBN 0684869020

Internet Sites

CBS Market Watch
www.CBSMarketWatch.com

Financial Planning Interactive
www.Financial-Planning.com

CNBC
www.CNBC.com

Morningstar
www.Morningstar.com

Association for Investment Management and Research
www.AIMR.org

Institute of Certified Financial Planners
www.CFP.net

Financial Advisor Magazine
www.FinancialAdvisorMagazine.com

Bloomberg
www.Bloomberg.com

Center for Asset Allocation
www.Frush.com/CAA

Yahoo Finance
Finance.Yahoo.com

Periodicals

Wall Street Journal
www.WSJ.com

Financial Times
www.FT.com

Kiplinger's Personal Finance
www.Kiplinger.com (800)-544-0155

Fortune
www.Fortune.com

Barron's
www.Barrons.com (800)-975-8620

Forbes
www.Forbes.com

Bloomberg Personal Finance
www.Bloomberg.com (609) 252-8352

Money
www.Money.com

The Economist
www.Economist.com

Smart Money
www.SmartMoney.com

Mutual Funds
www.MutualFundsMagazine.com

Worth
www.Worth.com

Red Herring
www.RedHerring.com

Business Week
www.BusinessWeek.com

Financial Analysts Journal
www.AIMRPubs.org

CFA Magazine
www.AIMRPubs.org

Journal of Financial Planning
www.fpanet.org/journal/

Appendix A:
Optimal Allocator

♦ ♦ ♦

Asset allocation is the strategy of dividing an investor's wealth among the different asset classes and asset subclasses to achieve the highest expected total rate of return for the given level of risk the investor is willing and able to assume. Empirical evidence has concluded that how you allocate your wealth, rather than which securities you select, determines the majority of your investment performance over time.

The Optimal Allocator is based on the Optimal Investing methodology and will help you determine your risk tolerance and help identify your target optimal asset mix. This worksheet presents a number of questions and based on your responses will suggest one of five target optimal asset mixes that may be the most appropriate for you. Each target optimal asset mix is designed to give you the highest expected total rate of return for the level of risk you are willing and able to assume.

The Optimal Allocator and Optimal Investing methodology were developed by the Frush Financial Group. The target optimal asset mixes should not be considered investment advice and should be considered within the context of all relevant investment strategies and when making investment decisions. Lastly, since your objectives and constraints may change over time, you may want to revisit this worksheet annually.

Optimal Allocator is a service of Frush Financial Group, LLC.

1 What is your investment goal?

[A] ☐ To make a purchase or pay an expense within 3 years using a substantial portion of my portfolio.

[B] ☐ To provide a source of current income (interest and dividends).

[C] ☐ To balance capital appreciation with current income.

[D] ☐ To emphasize capital appreciation over current income.

[E] ☐ To emphasize aggressive capital appreciation.

2 What is your age group?

[A] ☐ Under 39

[B] ☐ 40 – 49

[C] ☐ 50 – 59

[D] ☐ 60 – 69

[E] ☐ 70 and over

3 How much of your portfolio do you anticipate liquidating and using to make purchases within the next 5 years?

[A] ☐ 0%

[B] ☐ Between 1% – 15%

[C] ☐ Between 15% – 25%

[D] ☐ Between 25% – 50%

[E] ☐ Between 50% – 100%

4 Approximately what percentage of your total investment holdings does this portfolio represent?

[A] ☐ Under 25%
[B] ☐ Between 25% – 50%
[C] ☐ Between 50% – 75%
[D] ☐ Between 75% – 100%

5 How secure are your future sources of income (employment, investment, retirement)?

[A] ☐ Very secure
[B] ☐ Secure
[C] ☐ Balanced
[D] ☐ Not secure
[E] ☐ Very not secure

6 How strongly do you prefer securities with lower market value volatility and lower expected returns over securities with higher market value volatility and higher expected returns?

[A] ☐ Strongly prefer
[B] ☐ Prefer
[C] ☐ Indifferent
[D] ☐ Do not prefer
[E] ☐ Strongly do not prefer

7 When the market is doing well, do you prefer to sell less risky investments and buy more risky investments with the proceeds?

[A] ☐ Strongly prefer
[B] ☐ Prefer
[C] ☐ Indifferent
[D] ☐ Do not prefer
[E] ☐ Strongly do not prefer

8 The following chart illustrates potential gains and losses a portfolio may experience over the next 10-year period. Please select the potential gain or loss grouping most preferable to you.

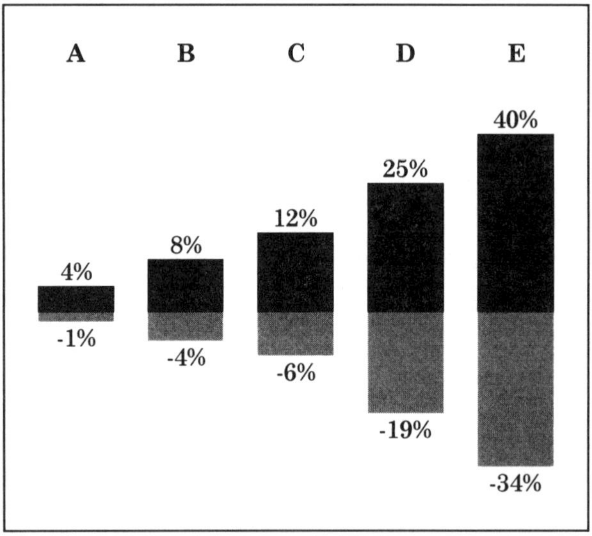

☐ A ☐ B ☐ C ☐ D ☐ E

9 About what percentage of your monthly net income is allocated to paying debt (not including your monthly mortgage payment on your principal residence)?

[A] ☐ Between 0% – 15%
[B] ☐ Between 15% – 25%
[C] ☐ Between 25% – 50%
[D] ☐ Between 50% – 100%

10 How many dependents do you financially support?

[A] ☐ None
[B] ☐ Between 1 – 3
[C] ☐ 4 or more

11 What is the size of your emergency fund?

[A] ☐ Do not have one
[B] ☐ Between 1 – 3 months of average monthly expenses
[C] ☐ Between 4 – 6 months of average monthly expenses
[D] ☐ More than 6 months of average monthly expenses

12 About what percentage of your retirement income do you anticipate coming from this portfolio?

[A] ☐ Between 0% – 15%
[B] ☐ Between 15% – 25%
[C] ☐ Between 25% – 50%
[D] ☐ Between 50% – 100%

13 What is your experience with equity investments?

[A] ☐ Extensive experience
[B] ☐ Moderate experience
[C] ☐ Very little experience
[D] ☐ No experience

14 What is your experience with fixed-income investments?

[A] ☐ Extensive experience
[B] ☐ Moderate experience
[C] ☐ Very little experience
[D] ☐ No experience

15 What is your experience with alternative investments (real estate, commodities, hedge funds)?

[A] ☐ Extensive experience
[B] ☐ Moderate experience
[C] ☐ Very little experience
[D] ☐ No experience

16 Please select ONE of the following that best describes your view on portfolio risk?

[A] ☐ I prefer investments with low risk.

[B] ☐ I mostly prefer investments with low risk, but I am willing to accept some investments with moderate risk.

[C] ☐ I prefer a balanced approach of low, moderate and high risk investments.

[D] ☐ I mostly prefer investments with high risk, but am willing to accept some investments with moderate and low risk.

[E] ☐ I prefer investments with high risk.

17 How much additional risk are you willing to assume to earn a higher expected total rate of return?

[A] ☐ I am willing to accept more risk with all of my investments to earn a higher expected total rate of return.

[B] ☐ I am willing to accept more risk with a portion of my investments to earn a higher expected total rate of return.

[C] ☐ I am willing to accept slightly more risk with all of my investments to earn a higher expected total rate of return.

[D] ☐ I am willing to accept slightly more risk with a portion of my investments to earn a higher expected total rate of return.

[E] ☐ I am not willing to accept more risk to earn a higher expected total rate of return.

SCORESHEET

For each number below, please circle the letter and score given how you answered the corresponding question from the aforementioned questions. A box at the end should be used to sum your score.

1	[A] **1**	[B] **3**	[C] **6**	[D] **9**	[E] **12**
2	[A] **12**	[B] **9**	[C] **6**	[D] **3**	[E] **1**
3	[A] **12**	[B] **9**	[C] **6**	[D] **3**	[E] **1**
4	[A] **10**	[B] **8**	[C] **6**	[D] **4**	
5	[A] **16**	[B] **13**	[C] **10**	[D] **7**	[E] **4**
6	[A] **2**	[B] **5**	[C] **8**	[D] **11**	[E] **14**
7	[A] **7**	[B] **6**	[C] **5**	[D] **4**	[E] **3**
8	[A] **1**	[B] **5**	[C] **9**	[D] **13**	[E] **17**
9	[A] **7**	[B] **5**	[C] **3**	[D] **1**	
10	[A] **5**	[B] **4**	[C] **3**		
11	[A] **2**	[B] **4**	[C] **6**	[D] **8**	
12	[A] **8**	[B] **6**	[C] **4**	[D] **2**	
13	[A] **5**	[B] **4**	[C] **3**	[D] **2**	
14	[A] **5**	[B] **4**	[C] **3**	[D] **2**	
15	[A] **5**	[B] **4**	[C] **3**	[D] **2**	

16	[A] **1**	[B] **5**	[C] **9**	[D] **13**	[E] **17**
17	[A] **13**	[B] **10**	[C] **7**	[D] **4**	[E] **1**

**Your
Sum of Points**

☐

33 - 58

If your score falls within the range of 33-58 you have a low risk tolerance and should emphasize aggressive capital preservation.

59 - 84

If your score falls within the range of 59-84 you have a low to moderate risk tolerance and should emphasize capital presser-vation with some growth.

85 - 121

If your score falls within the range of 85-121 you have a moderate risk tolerance and should emphasize a balanced approach to capital appreciation and capital preservation.

122 - 147

If your score falls within the range of 122-147 you have a moderate to high risk tolerance and should emphasize capital appreciation.

148 - 173

If your score falls within the range of 148-173 you have a high risk tolerance and should emphasize aggressive capital appreciation.

The following are five target optimal asset mixes that may be the most appropriate for you. Each target optimal asset mix is designed to give investors the highest expected total rate of return for the level of risk they are willing and able to assume.

SUGGESTED TARGET OPTIMAL ASSET MIXES

Points

33 - 58 **Aggressive Capital Preservation Portfolio**

Equities	25%
Fixed Income	50%
Cash & Equivalents	25%
Alternative Assets	0%

59 - 84 **Capital Preservation Portfolio**

Equities	40%
Fixed Income	40%
Cash & Equivalents	20%
Alternative Assets	0%

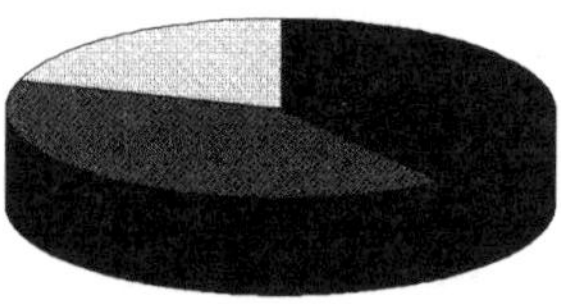

85 - 121

Balanced Portfolio

Equities	55%
Fixed Income	30%
Cash & Equivalents	10%
Alternative Assets	5%

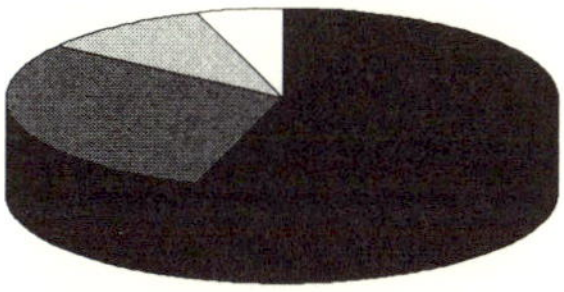

122 - 147

Capital Appreciation Portfolio

Equities	70%
Fixed Income	20%
Cash & Equivalents	5%
Alternative Assets	5%

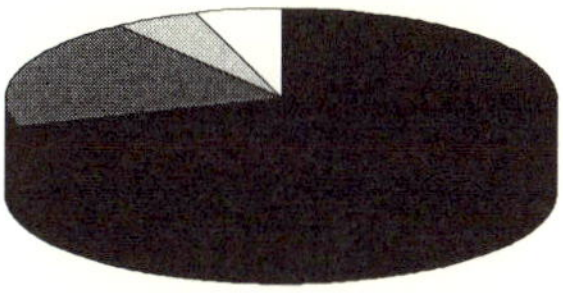

148 - 173

Aggressive Capital Appreciation Portfolio

Equities	80%
Fixed Income	5%
Cash & Equivalents	5%
Alternative Assets	10%

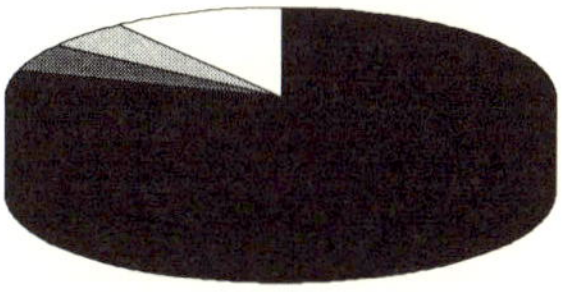

(END OF OPTIMAL ALLOCATOR)

Appendix B:
Optimal Portfolio Building Checklist

♦ ♦ ♦

The following action checklist will help you organize, structure and visualize the process of building your optimal portfolio. Specifically, this action checklist will help you to:

- Establish your objectives and constraints
- Design your optimal portfolio
- Draft your Investment Policy Statement
- Construct your optimal portfolio
- Monitor your optimal portfolio
- Rebalance your optimal portfolio

Establishing your objectives & constraints

☐ Determine your investment time horizon. Again, this is the period from the present to the future point in time when you will no longer need the assets in your portfolio.

☐ Make a list of all of your specific financial goals during your investment time horizon. Remember, they need to be realistic, achievable and measurable.

☐ Determine your risk tolerance, or how much portfolio volatility you are willing and able to assume in order to achieve your specific financial goals. Appendix A will help you determine your risk tolerance.

☐ Determine how much liquidity you will need during your investment time horizon. Will 5% of your portfolio's assets in income-oriented assets be sufficient to cover your cash need or will 10% or even 15% be more appropriate?

- [ ] Determine what tax issues may arise during your investment time horizon and identify how you will effectively address them. Consider hiring a CPA if the issues are numerous and/or complex.

- [ ] Determine what legal and regulatory issues may arise during your investment time horizon and identify how you will effectively address them. Estate planning attorneys and investment advisors can provide valuable insights if complex issues arise.

- [ ] Determine what, if any, unique circumstances and preferences you will need to address during your investment time horizon.

Designing your optimal portfolio

- [ ] Determine your optimal asset mix. Your optimal asset mix is based on your desired risk and return trade-off profile. To identify your profile, you will need to determine the level of risk you are willing and able to assume. A risk tolerance questionnaire may be the best way for you to determine your risk tolerance. A sound risk tolerance questionnaire will evaluate both your willingness and ability (or capacity) to tolerate risk. Appendix A of this book provides such a questionnaire.
    - ➡ Determine which asset classes to employ.
    - ➡ Determine how much to allocate to growth and value stocks.
    - ➡ Determine how much to allocate to small, mid, and large market capitalization stocks.
    - ➡ Determine the amount, if any, within each asset class you will allocate to international assets.
    - ➡ Determine how much to allocate within each asset class or asset subclass to match liquidity needs.
    - ➡ Determine how much to allocate to tax-exempt, if at all, and taxable securities.

- [ ] Establish your allocation ranges, or the acceptable range the percentage weighting of each asset class is permitted to move within without triggering rebalancing. Depending on the degree of discipline you wish to bring to the process, your allocation ranges can be narrow, moderate or wide.

- [ ] Determine whether your portfolio will be actively managed or passively managed.

- [ ] Identify which construction method or methods to employ. The primary methods include individual securities, separately management accounts, mutual funds and index investments. Your portfolio can be a combination of all methods if you so desire.

- [ ] Select your specific investments.

- [ ] Select your asset allocation strategy. Your options include either strategic or tactical.

Drafting your Investment Policy Statement

- [ ] Collect all essential financial documents, including your latest monthly investment statement, the objectives and constraints you identified in chapter five and the portfolio you designed in chapter six.

- [ ] Write the purpose of the IPS so that all interested parties know why you are using it.

- [ ] Develop and write an executive summary, including your objectives and constraints and key points addressed in the design of your optimal portfolio.

- [ ] Summarize your current portfolio.

- [ ] Outline the optimal portfolio you designed in the previous chapter. Here is where you include the asset classes and asset subclasses you will employ. In addition, you should include the percentage weightings for each, along with allocation range ceilings and floors.

- [ ] Outline how the portfolio manager shall construct your optimal portfolio. Your options include individual securities, separately managed accounts (wrap accounts, hedge funds and related), mutual funds and index investments.

- [ ] Outline how the portfolio manager shall monitor your optimal portfolio. Here you could list the benchmark or benchmarks you will evaluate performance against.

- ☐ Outline how the portfolio manager shall rebalance your optimal portfolio.
- ☐ Communicate the duties and responsibilities of the portfolio manager and yourself.
- ☐ Define the annual review procedures.
- ☐ Obtain a signature from the appropriate person at the investment firm and sign the document yourself.

Constructing your optimal portfolio

- ☐ Review and understand your Investment Policy Statement. Everything you need to implement should be contained within this document.
- ☐ Select a financial services firm (Ameritrade, Fidelity, Charles Schwab, Merrill Lynch, etc) that provides the services you desire at reasonable costs. Many investors may want to seek professional help rather than to implement their plan by themselves. Chapter thirteen of this book provides some insights into obtaining professional counsel as well as a list of questions to ask when evaluating an advisor. Although not always the case, the decision of which financial services firm to use has already been made and outlined in your Investment Policy Statement.
- ☐ Implement the plan as outlined in your Investment Policy Statement.

Monitoring your optimal portfolio

- ☐ Identify your current portfolio asset class weightings.
- ☐ Compare the current portfolio asset class weightings to your optimal asset mix and allocation ranges.
- ☐ Take notice of any deviations above or below the appropriate allocation range.
- ☐ Evaluate any deviation or deviations within the context of the asset allocation strategy employed (strategic or tactical).

- [ ] Proceed to rebalancing if any deviation or deviations are not appropriate given the asset allocation strategy employed (Note: proceeding to rebalancing does not implicitly mean the weightings in a portfolio must be adjusted since the costs of such an action must be weighed against the benefits).

- [ ] Go to step 1 and repeat the monitoring process.

Rebalancing your optimal portfolio

- [ ] Determine the amount of rebalancing that is needed. The typical amount is the difference between the current asset weighting and the weighting as defined by your optimal asset mix.

- [ ] Determine the cost basis for any assets that may need to be sold.

- [ ] Determine the costs (transaction and taxes) of selling the asset as determined in step 1.

- [ ] Evaluate whether or not the costs should delay the rebalancing transaction.

- [ ] If the impact of costs does not prove material, either sell or buy the appropriate amount, as determined in step 1.

- [ ] Depending on whether step 5 involved selling or buying, either determine which asset class or classes to sell to fund the purchase or determine which asset class or classes to buy with the proceeds from the asset sold.

- [ ] Reallocate as determined in step 6.

Glossary

♦ ♦ ♦

Active Management: A portfolio management strategy whereby the management of a portfolio is accomplished using the skills and judgment of an investor or portfolio manager. Active management attempts to beat the market by employing security selection and market timing.

Actual Return: The return an investor has realized, or one that has occurred in a past holding period. Actual returns are commonly annualized and expressed as percentages.

American Depository Receipts (ADRs): Stocks issued in the United States by large U.S. money center banks. Each ADR represents an ownership interest in a fixed number of shares of a foreign company. ADRs trade either on a U.S. exchange or over-the-counter and are denominated in U.S. dollars. They can be bought and sold like U.S. stocks and their dividends are paid in U.S. dollars.

Appreciation: The increase in the market value of an asset.

Asset: Anything of commercial value that can be sold for cash.

Asset Allocation: The strategy of dividing an investor's wealth among the different asset classes and asset subclasses to achieve the highest expected total rate of return.

Asset Allocation Strategy: Defines how and when a portfolio should be rebalanced given deviations of the portfolio's asset mix from its optimal asset mix. Also referred to as rebalancing strategy.

Asset Class: A group of securities that share similar underlying characteristics as well as very similar risk and return trade-off profiles. The four primary asset classes are equities, fixed-income, cash & equivalents and alternatives. Each asset class can be further divided into asset subclasses.

Beta: A measure of risk. The degree of security price volatility in relation to the overall market. Expressed as an absolute number rather than as a percentage.

Business Risk: Risk attributed to a company's operations, particularly those involving sales and income.

Call Risk: Risk attributed to an event where a security may be called prior to maturity resulting in a situation where the investor may not be able to reinvest the proceeds at the same or higher rate of return as the original investment. This risk is associated with bonds and preferred stock.

Called: The redemption or purchase of a security by the issuer before maturity.

Capital Gain: The difference between the market price of an asset and its purchase price.

Closed-End Fund: Closed-end funds are mutual funds in that they represent a pool of investments managed by a portfolio manager. In contrast to traditional mutual funds, closed-end funds are listed on U.S. exchanges and have a fixed number of shares outstanding. Their market prices are determined exclusively by investor demand.

Commission: A fee charged by a financial services firm to execute a buy or sell transaction.

Commodities: Tangible articles of trade, such as agricultural products or metals, which are indistinguishable and thus interchangeable with each other. Commodities are processed and resold.

Constraints: Parameters and limitations that must be adhered to when designing, constructing, monitoring and rebalancing a portfolio.

Convertible: A provision often attached to preferred stock that gives the owner the option to convert, or exchange, his or her preferred shares into a fixed number of common stock shares after a predetermined date. The market value of this type of preferred is more volatile since its value is influenced by the market value of the underlying common stock.

Correlation: The technical term used to measure how closely the prices of two assets move together over time.

Country Risk: Risk that macroeconomic or political events will negatively impact the market value of an international investment.

Cumulative Preferred: A preferred stock that has priority in receiving dividends over that of common stock. The cumulative provision obligates the corporation to pay all accumulated dividends before dividends can be made to the shareholders of common stock.

Diversification: A strategy designed to reduce total risk by combining a large number of securities within a particular asset class that exhibit similar risk and return trade-off profiles.

Dividend: A taxable distribution to common and preferred shareholders from of a corporation's profits.

Earnings Per Share: A corporation's earnings divided by the total number of shares that corporation has outstanding.

Efficient Frontier: All possible optimal portfolio combinations where the expected rate of return is maximized given the specific level of risk assumed. Usually illustrated as a curved line within the risk-return graph.

Efficient Market Hypothesis: The theory that says security prices are fair and reasonable because they fully reflect all available public and non-public information that might impact them.

Equity: Ownership interest in a publicly or privately held asset, such as a corporation.

Exchange-Traded Fund: A closed-end fund that is managed in such a way as to match its return to that of a specific underlying index, such as the S&P 500 or the Dow Jones Industrials Average.

Expected Return: A forecast of what an investor will earn, both appreciation and income (dividends and interest), in a future holding period. Commonly expressed as an annualized percentage.

Financial Risk: The risk attributed to a company's financial stability and structure, namely the company's use of debt to leverage earnings. Companies that use more debt are considered more risky.

Fixed-Income Security: A security that represents a loan to a corporation or governmental entity in order to raise capital. Moreover, they are debt instruments that obligate an issuer to make periodic interest payments to the purchaser on predetermined dates in predetermined amounts until the security reaches maturity or is called by the issuer.

Growth Company: A company that generates rates of return far in excess of their weighted average cost of capital. This allows most growth companies to generate higher rates of return on their invested capital than their peers.

Growth Stock: A common stock that appreciates faster than the common stocks of its industry peers.

Index: A statistical measure of the total market values for a group of similar securities. Examples include the Dow Jones Industrial Average and the S&P 500.

Index Fund: A mutual fund that is managed in such a way as to match its return to that of a specific underlying index, such as the S&P 500.

Industry Risk: Risk attributed to a group of companies within a particular industry due to events within that group.

Investment Policy Statement (IPS): A written document that outlines an investor's financial plan, including the designing, constructing, monitoring and rebalancing phases. An IPS serves as a blueprint for building an optimal portfolio.

Investment Style: Defines whether the portfolio will emphasize growth or value securities.

Inflation: The across-the-board increase in asset market values. The opposite is deflation.

Intrinsic Value: The perceived value of an asset, regardless of the actual market value.

Legal and Regulatory Considerations: Regulations and laws that an investor and portfolio manager are obligated to follow.

Liquidity: The ability of an asset to be converted quickly into cash and its equivalents.

Liquidity Needs: The degree to which an investor requires cash and its equivalents to support everyday activities and special purchases.

Liquidity Risk: Risk attributed to an investor's ability to buy or sell a security in the secondary market near market prices.

Management Fees: Fees charged to investors by professional portfolio managers for their services. Typically expressed as a percentage of assets under management.

Management Style: Defines whether the management of the portfolio will emphasize passive or active management.

Market Capitalization: The total market value of a publicly traded company. Calculated by multiplying the number of shares outstanding by the market price per share.

Market Portfolio: A hypothetical portfolio comprising every possible investable security.

Market Timing: The strategy of determining when to purchase or sell a security.

Market Value: The price of a security as determined by purchasers and sellers in a free and open market. Typically expressed as the last reported transaction price.

Maturity: The date on which an issuer is obligated to pay the principal from a fixed-income security to the purchaser.

Modern Portfolio Theory: Says that investors and portfolio managers should not evaluate each security on a stand-alone basis. Rather, each security should be evaluated based on its ability to enhance the overall risk and return trade-off profile of the portfolio. Sets the tone for investing according to the desired risk and return trade-off profile.

Monitoring: The process of evaluating and comparing a portfolio's asset allocation mix to both the optimal asset mix and allocation ranges. In addition, monitoring can also involve comparing the portfolio's performance to a benchmark or benchmarks.

Mutual Fund: An investable pool of securities managed by a professional portfolio manager. Mutual funds offer investors significant liquidity, a diversified investment and low initial minimums.

Net Asset Value: The value of a mutual fund share. Calculated by subtracting the liabilities of a mutual fund from its assets and then dividing by the total number of mutual funds shares outstanding.

Objectives: Term used in the investment field to represent an investor's return aspiration, such as protecting capital or receiving current income, and his or her tolerance for risk.

Optimal Asset Mix: The appropriate asset classes and asset subclasses an investor allocates his or her portfolio assets to in order to produce the desired risk and return trade-off profile.

Optimal Investing: The strategy of employing time-honored and research backed principles and practices to protect and grow an investor's wealth within the context of his or her object ives and constraints.

Optimal Portfolio: A portfolio with the highest expected total rate of return given the specific level of risk an investor is willing and able to assume in order to achieve his or her specific financial goals.

Passive Management: Management style where a portfolio is invested using index investments. Passive management attempts to match the performance of a portfolio to that of an underlying market index.

Portfolio: A group of investments typically owned by the same person or organization.

Price-To-Book Ratio: A valuation measure for common stocks. Calculated by dividing a common stock's market price by its book value.

Price-To-Earnings Ratio: A valuation measure for common stocks. Calculated by dividing a common stock's total market capitalization by its total net earnings over the last twelve months.

Real Estate Investment Trust (REIT): A trust that raises money from shareholders and invests the money in property and/or mortgages. Federal regulations stipulate 95% of earnings must flow to shareholders.

Realized Capital Gain: Appreciation that is taxable since the underlying investment was sold.

Rebalancing: The process of selling and buying investments in order to return the current asset class weightings to the optimal asset mix.

Regulation Risk: Risk that new laws and regulations will negatively impact the market value of an investment.

Reinvestment Risk: Risk that interest or dividends received by a shareholder for holding a security will not earn expected rates of return due to falling interest rates during the holding period.

Risk: Uncertainty that an investment's actual return will not match its expected return.

Risk and Return Trade-Off Profile: A measure of the relationship between a portfolio's expected rate of return and its expected risk.

Risk Tolerance: The degree of risk an investor is willing and able to assume to make an investment.

Risk-Free Rate: The return earned by a shareholder from investing in U.S. Treasury Bills, or what are considered riskless investments.

Securities and Exchange Commission: The federal governing agency that regulates the investment field.

Security: An investable asset, excluding insurance policies, fixed annuities and futures contracts, which can be bought and sold.

Security Selection: The strategy of determining which securities to buy or sell. Commonly referred to as stock picking.

Sharpe Ratio: Method developed by William F. Sharpe to measure the risk-adjusted return of an investment or portfolio. Calculates the amount of excess return per unit of risk.

Standard Deviation: One of the best measures of risk for an investment. Technically speaking, it is the degree to which actual returns are spread around the mean actual return. Expressed as a percentage.

Strategic Asset Allocation: A rebalancing strategy whereby the asset classes within a portfolio generally are rebalanced when their weightings either move above their allocation range ceilings or below their allocation range floors.

Systematic Risk: Risk resulting from conditions, events and trends occurring outside the scope of the investment. The four principle types of systematic risk include exchange rate risk, interest rate risk, market risk and purchasing power risk.

Tactical Asset Allocation: A market timing strategy whereby the portfolio's optimal asset mix and allocation ranges are intentionally changed with the goal of capturing short-term profits.

Tax Consideration: The attention that is given to realizing, deferring or avoiding taxes.

Tax-Equivalent Yield: The yield you would receive given your tax rate if the income from your fixed-income security were taxable.

Time Horizon: The length of time an investor plans to make an investment. Also referred to as time period and holding period.

Total Return: The total return earned by a shareholder for making an investment. Calculated by summing appreciation and income (dividends and interest) received and dividing by the initial investment. Typically expressed as an annualized percentage.

Turnover: A measure of how much a portfolio's investments have changed over a certain period of time, such as one year. Expressed as a percentage share of a portfolio that is sold during a specific time period. The higher the turnover percentage, the greater the trading activity.

Unique Circumstances and Preferences: Incorporates anything that cannot be categorized in one of the other four constraint categories. One example is an unusual preference an investor has that in some way impairs the portfolio management process.

Unrealized Capital Gain: Appreciation that is not taxable since the underlying investment has not been sold.

Unsystematic Risk: Risk that is unique to an investment, such as business risk, financial risk, industry risk, liquidity risk, call risk, and regulation risk. Diversification can minimize, if not eliminate altogether, unsystematic risk.

Value Stock: Common stock that is considered undervalued given the current stock price and its expected rate of return.

Volatility: The movement either up or down, in the price of a security.

Yield: The annual rate of return determined by dividing the annual interest payments by the purchase price (or current market value depending on the purpose of the analysis).

Yield Curve: A graphical representation of the relationship between fixed-income yields and their time to maturity.

Index

♦ ♦ ♦

N

O

W

Y

Z

About the Author

Scott P. Frush, CFA, CFP, is an accomplished investment advisor and expert in asset allocation theory and its application to the design, construction, and management of optimal investment portfolios. His unique methodology, best described as a combination between principle-based niche investing and process-oriented investing, is known as Optimal Investing.

For more than a decade, Scott Frush has helped investors protect and grow their investment portfolios for powerful results. Mr. Frush is President of Bloomfield Hills, Michigan, based Frush Financial Group, a signature provider of wealth management services to affluent and ultra affluent individuals and families. His firm has built a reputation for building, protecting and growing optimal portfolios utilizing the Optimal Investing methodology. In addition, Mr. Frush is Director and founder of the Center for Asset Allocation, a research organization whose mission is to educate, promote and assist investors with asset allocation theory and its application to the management of their investment portfolios.

Mr. Frush earned his Master of Business Administration degree in finance from the University of Notre Dame and his Bachelor of Business Administration degree in finance from Eastern Michigan University. He holds the Chartered Financial Analyst (CFA) and Certified Financial Planner (CFP) designations and is a member of the Investment Analysts Society of Detroit and the Association for Investment Management & Research.

About Frush Financial Group

Frush Financial Group is a Registered Investment Advisor and provider of private wealth management services to affluent and ultra affluent individuals and families. Our singular focus is to build, protect and grow our clients' wealth, while delivering exceptional and unparalleled service. We are a client-first organization committed to upholding the highest standards of professional excellence, integrity and ethical behavior.

The hallmark and distinction of Frush Financial Group is our expertise in asset allocation theory and portfolio application. This expertise, together with our client-first philosophy, empowers us to protect and grow our clients' most important assets.

Frush Financial Group designs, constructs and manages investment portfolios using our proprietary Optimal Investing methodology. We utilize individual securities, managed accounts, mutual funds and index investments. We provide objecttive and customized investment management solutions uncompromised by sales commissions or the use of proprietary investment products. In addition, we also offer risk management and trust and private foundation establishment and management.

Frush Financial Group
37000 Woodward Avenue, Suite 101
Bloomfield Hills, Michigan 48304

(248) 642-6800

www.Frush.com